SPEAKING *of*
DANCE

SPEAKING *of* DANCE

Twelve Contemporary Choreographers on Their Craft

JOYCE MORGENROTH

ROUTLEDGE
NEW YORK AND LONDON

Published in 2004 by
Routledge
Taylor & Francis Group
270 Madison Avenue
New York, NY 10016
www.routledge-ny.com

Published in Great Britain by
Routledge
Taylor & Francis Group
2 Park Square
Milton Park, Abingdon
Oxon OX14 4RN
www.routledge.co.uk

10 9 8 7 6 5 4 3 2 1

Library of Congress Cataloging-in-Publication Data
    Morgenroth, Joyce, 1945-
      Speaking of dance: twelve contemporary choreographers on their craft / by Joyce Morgenroth.
        p. cm.
      Includes bibliographical references and index.
      ISBN 0-415-96798-8 (hb : alk. paper) —ISBN 0-415-96799-6 (pb : alk. paper)
      1. Choreography. 2. Choreographers—United States—Biography. I. Title.

    GV1782.5.M67 2004
    792.8'2—dc22   2004019115

Contents

List of Illustrations

Merce Cunningham
1. Merce Cunningham at the computer (photo Edward Santalone)
2. Rehearsal of *Second Hand* by Merce Cunningham, with John Cage at piano (photo James Klosty)
3. *Field and Figures* by Merce Cunningham (photo Tom Brazil)

Anna Halprin
1. Anna Halprin in *Memories from My Closet* (photo Julie Lemberger)
2. Rehearsal of *Esposizione* by Anna Halprin (photographer unknown)
3. Anna Halprin in *Apartment 6* (photographer unknown)

David Gordon
1. David Gordon in *My Folks* (photo Chris Ha)
2. *The Mysteries & What's So Funny* by David Gordon (photo Andrew Eccles)
3. *Chair* by David Gordon (photo Lois Greenfield)

Trisha Brown
1. Trisha Brown (photo Lois Greenfield)
2. *Set and Reset* by Trisha Brown (photo Chris Callis)
3. *Five Part Weather Invention* by Trisha Brown (photo Chris Callis)

Lucinda Childs
1. Lucinda Childs (photo Kishin Shinoyama)
2. Chart of *Radial Courses* by Lucinda Childs
3. *One and One* by Lucinda Childs (photo Peter Perazio)
4. *Concerto* by Lucinda Childs (photo Peter Perazio)

Acknowledgments

Ann McCutchan's wonderful collection of interviews with composers, *The Muse That Sings*, inspired me to write this book; her comments on my manuscript helped me shape my editing and writing. My profound thanks go to Phyllis Kantar, who read every interview and relentlessly coaxed me toward clarity, and to Jane Mushabac, whose astute response to the introductory sections got me on track. Two leaves of absence granted by Cornell University enabled me to travel and write; Arthur Morgenroth and his family provided an ever-delightful New York home. Thanks to my husband Gerald Wolfe for his calm support and his patience when I was on the road or virtually wedded to the computer. I'm indebted to my editor Richard Carlin for having taken on this project and for ushering it along, to Amy Villarejo and Andrea Hammer for brainstorming titles with me, and to my students Kathleya Afanador and Eugenia Chun for bibliographic research. During the years of putting this book together I've relied on and greatly appreciated the company managers and staff who responded to my queries. Special thanks go to David Vaughan, Merce Cunningham's archivist, who graciously met with me when I needed more information. My deepest gratitude of all goes to the choreographers for their brilliant work and for the time they generously gave to this project.

Introduction

Watching dance fills me with consummate satisfaction. I love the ebb and flow of a Mark Morris canon as it washes me in eddies of movement; the fitful sidestepping of four Trisha Brown dancers trying to stay directly behind a fifth dancer's unpredictable, slippery progress across the stage; and the startling moment when Ann Carlson, engulfed in layers of old ladies' clothing and taking a first shuffling step, cries like a newborn baby. These choreographers—and others equally inspired—are masters of movement, form, and theater. Because I am also a dancer and choreographer, I can't help feeling envy (I wish I had done that…), but even more, pride (This is what dance can be!). Drawn to the choreographers who had made such surprising, powerful dances, I wanted to talk with them, to find out how they make their work and how they experience their lives as choreographers. My conversations with them became this book.

Every step toward bringing *Speaking of Dance* into existence had its labors and its delights. Decades of going to performances in theaters, lofts, and public parks showed me what was out there and whetted my appetite to see more. Numerous trips to the New York Public Library Dance Collection at Lincoln Center allowed me to view recordings of dances I had missed seeing live. For six hours at a stretch in front of a video monitor, barely able to discern the movement because of the dim stage lighting, I struggled to perceive what the dances must have been. I read books, articles, reviews, and interviews. I became familiar with the voice of each choreographer even before we talked together. My interviews began in the fall of 2000 with Elizabeth Streb, whom I had known as a fellow dancer in New York in the 1970s, and ended with a trip to California in the spring of 2003, where I met the ebullient, ageless Anna Halprin.

1

I spoke to the choreographers in their lofts, living rooms, kitchens, and offices. I met two of them in the midst of their touring. Certain questions I asked frequently: how they got started as dancers and choreographers, what were their daily routines, and what collaborations had been important to them. I also asked about the emotional ups and downs they experience in making new work, whether they start a new piece by moving or by thinking, and how much they revise. My question about *why* they choreograph seemed to baffle some of them; but the answer inevitably emerged, even if not in direct response to my question. The ones who love to tell a good story, like David Gordon and Eiko Otake, didn't need many questions. They recounted tales of friends who encouraged them toward dance careers and of family members who were their artistic allies. Almost everyone had something to say about difficulties getting funding and the relief at seeing a dance finished. After talking with the choreographers, I transcribed the taped interviews, then organized and edited them into monologues, keeping their individual voices intact. Finally, the choreographers approved or made adjustments to what I had written. I am grateful for the time they generously gave to this project in the midst of exceedingly busy schedules and for the pleasure I had in being immersed in their words and work. They all were gracious and, as is evident, highly articulate.

No philosophy, style, or method unites these choreographers into a common pursuit, except that all are adventurers and visionaries. Their work is as different from each other's as a gurgling stream is from a torrent, as a crossword puzzle is from a poem. Cumulatively they have changed the face of dance precisely because as individuals they have ventured out and invented previously unimagined ways of making and presenting dances. They've made movement that is weighted, flung, elusive, pristine. They've made dances for intimate loft spaces, parking lots, and opera houses; for trained dancers, nondancers, and animals; in rehearsal clothes, costumed, and nude; with music, sounds, speech, and silence. They've made work alone or with collaborators, for their own companies and for other groups. They've found inspiration to suit their own intellects and passions. Witness Merce Cunningham's unquenchable fascination with movement, Lucinda Childs's methodical exploration of geometrical patterns, Meredith Monk's quest along a spiritual path, or Bill T. Jones's desire to change the world. Almost all those I interviewed first trained as dancers and began their professional lives as performers. Without knowing what might come of it, almost all converged on New York City where they walked the same downtown streets and climbed familiar worn-out warehouse stairs up to rented rehearsal spaces.

The pressure of being a choreographer is that you can't "write" a dance and then pass it on to be read or interpreted by someone else. A dance must be ushered from its first steps, through the teaching and rehearsal process, to the full performance, always dealing with a miscellany of people and with deadlines that are absolute. Then someone must continue to keep the repertory alive. Choreographers intimately depend on their dancers, but also on managers, musicians, designers, producers, and audiences. Making a dance takes a kind of courage not needed in most professions. On a daily basis it requires physical effort, imagination, and some deep confidence that the pieces will finally pull together. The choreographers in this book talk about the routines that help keep their work flowing. After decades of choreographing, some think about how to keep the process from getting stale. Choreographing is hard work, but they all relish that challenge. Elizabeth Streb talked about how "you get to invent the means of asking the questions that interest you. I don't think there's anything better." Or, as John Jasperse put it, "Can you believe that this is what we do for a living? We go into the room and we spend hours doing crazy, weird shit. That's great."

These choreographers have struggled with insufficient funding, the loss of dancers, the rigors of touring, and the general indifference of the populace at large. But they have also been recognized for their talents and productivity. All of the major dance honors have been given to them, including fellowships from the John Simon Guggenheim Foundation and the National Endowment for the Arts, New York Dance and Performance Awards (Bessies), and honorary doctorates. Half of them were selected from among the most creative people in the country—in any discipline—to receive prestigious MacArthur Foundation "Genius" Awards. In the short bios that precede each interview I give a sampling of their honors. Readers may refer to *Fifty Contemporary Choreographers*, edited by Martha Bremser, or to the choreographers' web pages, where, for the majority of them, a more complete record of awards and a list of their dances can also be found. Since all the choreographers in this book are actively making and showing their work, I refer you, above all, to the live performance of their dances.

When Trisha Brown's dancers continue dancing into the wings, not as a way to make a graceful exit but as a way to make us wonder about where the stage ends and where life begins; when Bill T. Jones teaches his dance *Table* to a group of six neighborhood men and to a group of six young girls and shows us both versions back to back; when Merce Cunningham at age eighty-four oversees onstage four throws of the die that will determine the arrangements of costumes, music, décor, and sections of his dance *Split*

Sides; when Mark Morris portrays the two female lead roles in *Dido and Aeneas* and makes us laugh and cry in quick succession; when Elizabeth Streb makes a dance consisting of a goggled dancer diving headlong through a sheet of glass, what can we do but cry, "La danse est morte! Vive la danse!"

Historical Background

Rebellion and exploration have been virtually a tradition since the inception of modern dance. Dating back to the first decades of the twentieth century, early modern dance choreographer Isadora Duncan rejected ballet's verticality and grace and made dances based on the wavelike movements of nature; not much later Ruth St. Denis created an exotic movement vocabulary that balanced precariously between sensuality and religion. By the 1930s Martha Graham was developing a dance technique whose angularity and sharp impulses expressed the psychological landscape while Doris Humphrey's fall and recovery technique emphasized the drama of the body off center. Despite these new styles of movement, the premises underlying the construction of a dance still followed centuries-long standards. We see them spelled out in mid-century composition primers. Humphrey's 1959 *The Art of Making Dances* taught choreographic craft by mapping out the strong and weak parts of the stage and showing how to manipulate the elements of gesture, design, dynamics, and rhythm. Two other influential dance composition texts of the period were written by Graham's adviser and music director, Louis Horst, who believed that dance, like music, must adhere to given forms. Dancers may have been spiraling dramatically to the floor, but they were doing so in orderly formations and in time to music.

Around the middle of the twentieth century, however, when Eastern philosophies were arousing interest in the Western world and modern art was exploring the flatness of the canvas and the materiality of paint, modern dance was being reinvented. By attending to the visual arts, philosophy, and technology, choreographers were discovering not just new ways to move, but new ways to conceive of what a dance was. The "art of making dances" was on the verge of a revolution.

Just as Einstein's theory of relativity exploded the dominant assumptions of his time, a few seminal figures gave a seismic jolt to American dance. In midcentury, two pivotal innovators, Merce Cunningham in New York and Anna Halprin in California, veered off from established standards of what dance should be. They asked every possible question. How does one go about making a dance? What form should a dance take? What sorts of movement can be done in performance? By what sorts of people? What about the choice of music and its relationship to the dance? Where can performances be held? What is expected of the audience? Does dance necessarily involve technique or can it be based on the presentation of ordinary behavior? Cunningham and Halprin brought such a host of radically new ideas to dancemaking that the effects of their innovations are still being explored.

The fifty-year collaboration between Merce Cunningham and the composer John Cage drew on Cage's interest in Zen philosophy and Cunningham's deep curiosity about movement. As a composer, Cage was an experimenter interested in sounds and silence rather than instrumental music, in duration rather than pulse, and in discovering ways to choose and organize sounds without regard to his personal tastes. Chance operations provided him with a system for generating unforeseen possibilities. Identifying the locations of imperfections in a sheet of paper or throwing yarrow sticks to select hexagrams in the ancient Chinese *I Ching* were means for determining pitches, their duration, and their source. Such chance methods freed Cage to organize sounds and silence in ways that were not bound by traditional—or even contemporary—compositional means.

In his desire to open up the possibilities of what could happen in a dance, Cunningham too used chance operations, in his case to determine the order, timing, and placement in space of movement phrases and to choose which dancers would perform each phrase. In this way, he separated his choreography from the dramatic premises of cause and effect and from personal movement habits. He valued any process that provided new options he wouldn't have thought of otherwise.

Cage and Cunningham upset the age-old intimacy between music and dance by establishing them as mutually independent, coexisting in time but with no moment-to-moment predetermined relationships. They left it up to the audience members to make their own connections. Cunningham also showed that the use of the stage space could be far more complex than it had been. Inspired by Einstein's statement that "there are no fixed points in space," he saw that more than one event could be in the space at a time and made dances with several modules of activity occurring simultaneously on stage, each having its own center. The effect on choreographic use of space was akin to the realization that the sun did not circle the earth—and caused as much uproar.

In the late 1950s John Cage taught composition at the New School for Social Research in New York City and also, briefly, to some Cunningham dance company members interested in his new methods. When the dancers wanted him to continue with the classes, he asked the composer Robert Ellis Dunn, who had taken some of his seminars, to teach them in his stead. Dunn agreed and offered dance composition courses starting in 1960. In his assignments (which could be as open-ended as "make a three-minute dance"), Dunn encouraged the class to create written scores that would define the parameters of the dance. Movements often were not set; they might be made according to a list of verbal instructions or as a spontaneous response to the bodily shifts made by whoever happened to be sitting and watching. Timings could be cued by the changing signals of a traffic light seen outside the studio window. Class discussion never assessed good and bad, but focused on the methods, materials, and structures used in making the dance. What a contrast to Louis Horst's set formulas for how to compose! The combination of Dunn's nonjudgmental teaching style and the extraordinary group of students taking the class created a flash point in the history of dance.

A few of the dancers involved in these classes and the Judson Memorial Church performances that emerged from them had come from the West Coast where they had been exposed to another radical innovator, Anna Halprin. As early as the 1950s Halprin used improvisation to elicit individualized movement from her dancers and gave them tasks to accomplish on stage: "Build a scaffold and then climb to the top." Her work combined nondancers performing together with trained dancers. She invaded parts of the theater previously unused or considered off-limits. On stage, her dancers moved upwards, hanging from a cargo net. In the theater house, they climbed over and through the audience. She ventured into nontheater environments, making dances on the mountain, by the ocean, and in the streets of San Francisco. Underlying her work was the use of scores. Sequences of diagrammed instructions—rather than arrangements of steps—were the basis for making dances. Through those who had worked with her, including Yvonne Rainer and Trisha Brown, her ideas were brought East to New York City and to Robert Ellis Dunn's classes.

In 1962, in order to show work made in these classes, the students arranged to perform at the Judson Memorial Church on Washington Square in Greenwich Village. It was the first of many concerts at that location. When the sequence of Dunn's composition classes ended later that year, the Judson artists met weekly in a workshop format and continued to perform new work. They collaborated with visual artists and composers who were adventurers in their own disciplines. Built structures, film projections, and ordinary objects were incorporated into performances. Dancers lugged mattresses around, piled them up, and dove onto them. In her piece *Carnation*, Lucinda Childs methodically wrapped hair curlers in sponges and stuffed them one by one into a collapsible salad colander inverted on her head. David Gordon talked his way through his *Random Breakfast*, improvising movement in the guise of one modern dance style after another. Meredith Monk invented singing techniques evocative of Middle Eastern chant, children's taunts, and tribal ululations, and devised a gestural language to accompany her voice. Bodies, trained or not, were dancing, clambering, walking, and gesticulating.

In a world of possibilities opened up by Cunningham, Cage, Halprin, and others, the dancers who were showing new work at the Judson Memorial Church broke every tenet of traditional modern dance—intentionally and with abandon. Myriad ideas—about performance, scale, technique, the body, society, and politics—were getting acted out polemically and entertainingly and every way in between. Nothing was out of bounds, not even occasional classical ballet steps.

Toward the end of the sixties, Yvonne Rainer used her ongoing work, *Continuous Project-Altered Daily*, to explore the purposeful blurring of distinctions between rehearsal, run-through, and performance and between choreographer and dancer. She questioned the very nature of performance: At what point does material in preparation become performable material? What sort of persona should the performer embody? Where do we draw the line between ordinary behavior and performance behavior? As Rainer made the process more democratic, passing the decision making increasingly onto the dancers, the group evolved and in 1970 became the improvisational performance group Grand Union. Having abandoned the distinction between choreographer and performer, the dancers were responsible for devising their own actions. Inevitably their improvisations began to crossbreed with their choreography. Trisha Brown, whose verbal wit contributed to Grand Union performances, added to her existing solo *Accumulation* the simultaneous narration of two intercut stories.

Overflowing from the Judson, performances took place in galleries and museums, down the sides of buildings, and in city streets. Audiences were among, surrounding, below, or above the performers. Pedestrian movement coexisted alongside of technical dance; sounds coexisted with music. Some pieces were so pared down that even movement itself had been stripped away; some pieces were bedecked not only with a charged physicality, but with pillows, platforms, screens, ladders, mats, you name it. A collection of dancers and choreographers working mostly in lower Manhattan welcomed a concatenation of old and new, high and low, East and West in a prodigious mixture that came to be called "postmodern."

New dancers arriving in New York kept feeding the pot. In the 1970s Eiko and Koma, whose roots were in the starkness of Japanese and German expressionist dance, began to develop a style that would lead to their ultraslow movement. Elizabeth Streb, skeptical of dance steps and inspired by the circus, devised challenging physical tasks, eventually leading her to bodily feats of flight and collision. Bill T. Jones and Arnie Zane brought their experience with contact improvisation and a penchant for political engagement. Mark Morris made profoundly musical, classically structured dances tinged with iconoclasm and the rhythms of Balkan folk dance and Flamenco. In the 1980s, nearly two decades after the Judson era, Ann Carlson, in a quest for a genuine language of gesture, sought out nondancers—human and animal—in order to use them and their natural movements in performance. In a different sort of return to the reality of movement, John Jasperse explored the weight of bodies encountering each other and bumping up against their separate intentions.

If these choreographers went counter to the standards and expectations of the dance world instead of joining the mainstream, why then have they come to be so well known? Why do they tour the world and why is their work produced in theaters and opera houses? Dance critic Edwin Denby recognized Cunningham's brilliance from his first 1944 concert. The Judson performances had Jill Johnston of *The Village Voice* and Allen Hughes of *The New York Times* as advocates. When the Brooklyn Academy of Music (BAM) initiated its Next Wave Festival in 1981 it sought out the vitality of these experimentalists. By offering funds for them to collaborate with important visual artists and composers, BAM spurred choreographers whose work had been shown primarily in alternative spaces to make new work on a bigger scale. Although the transition was not immediately successful, before long, new work by these choreographers grew to fit the proscenium stage. After having upended the old theatricality, the "next wave" of choreographers evolved a new theatricality that could coexist with the pleasures of the grand theater. The ballet world—better funded, better attended, but less well endowed with new ideas—sought out the energy and vision of these choreographers, interbreeding traditional technique with radical approaches to dancemaking. Opera companies in Europe and America commissioned their work, integrating nonclassical movement into the world of music.

The explosion of ideas that began in the mid-twentieth century hasn't stopped spewing out new methods, new movements, new contexts. While the work of these choreographers has matured, it has kept its edge of risk and surprise. As Cunningham said, one keeps finding "more possibilities which were always there; it's just that one's own mind hasn't seen them." These choreographers continue to propel dance forward. They continue to make history.

1
Merce Cunningham (b. 1919)

Merce Cunningham grew up in Centralia, Washington, where he studied dance with Maude Barrett. From her he learned tap dance and soft shoe, exhibition ballroom, and ethnic styles and had many opportunities to perform. After a year at George Washington University, he attended the Cornish School in Seattle, where he studied dance and theater and met John Cage, who was to be his lifelong collaborator. Cunningham went to New York in 1939 and joined Martha Graham's dance company as a soloist. In 1945 he left Graham's company, focused on choreographing, and in 1953 formed the Merce Cunningham Dance Company. Cunningham developed a dance technique that serves his choreography. Based on an upright posture with a flexible spine that can curve, arch, and twist, his technique emphasizes articulation, quickness, and the ability to change directions at any moment. His Westbeth Studio in New York's West Village continues to be a prominent center for dance training.

Merce Cunningham has been a prolific choreographer for sixty years and has been arguably the most influential choreographer of the twentieth century (see the Historical Background section). As he modestly puts it, "Dance has been what's interested me all my life." He believes that movement itself is complete and needs no overlay of emotion or intention. Chance operations, the means by which decisions are made via a randomized method, have served Cunningham's purposes, allowing him to establish the order of phrases, the choice of dancers, timings, and location in space without being limited by his own movement habits or dependent on dramatic narrative. Cunningham has collaborated with contemporary musicians and artists including Jasper Johns and Robert Rauschenberg.

He has also made dances for film and video that take advantage of the camera's different spatial perspective. In the last decade he has used the DanceForms (formerly LifeForms) program as a way to devise new movement possibilities on the computer.

Merce Cunningham has received high honors from France, Italy, Sweden, England, and Spain. In America he was given the MacArthur "Genius" Award, the Dorothy and Lillian Gish Prize, New York Dance and Performance (Bessie) Awards, John Simon Guggenheim Fellowships, the National Medal of Arts, the Dance/USA National Honor, the Samuel H. Scripps Award for Lifetime Contribution to Dance, and Kennedy Center Honors, among others, and was inducted into the National Museum of Dance Hall of Fame. He has been granted honorary doctorates from Wesleyan University and the University of Illinois.

* * *

Merce Cunningham at the computer (photo Edward Santalone)

Merce Cunningham

Way back a long, long time ago I began to work with some dancers. It was the 1950s. I didn't have any money and I certainly couldn't pay anybody since I was barely surviving myself, so I tried to think of what I could give the dancers in return for their labors. I thought, well, maybe teaching class. So I rented a studio for about a dollar an hour where we could get together and I would give class. The class was used as a laboratory, as a way to try out movement material. It also helped develop a common vocabulary. I had tried working with dancers from other techniques or styles, both ballet and the existing styles of modern dance, and I could see it didn't work. Then when we had enough time to rehearse, we would work on a dance. That's how it started and then it just kept up.

There were six dancers in the beginning, including myself, and we worked closely together. There are more of them now, which makes it more complicated to be with each one of them. I try to still see them as individual dancers as much as I can. Nonetheless, I think the relationship between me and my dancers is more formal these days than in the past. I don't know if the dancers are scared exactly—of me or the work. I know there's always a risk on both sides when beginning something new, particularly because of the way we work in my company. But the work goes on between us.

These days I give the company class and so do my assistant Robert Swinston and others. That's very much a part of our routine. When we're on tour of course it's hard to get up the morning after a show and do a class, but it's always better if you do. I remember once Ulysses Dove, who was with our company and then later with the Ailey Company, complained about class on tour. I said, "But Ulysses, isn't it better with it than without?" and he admitted, "You're right." I know our dancers want class. It's a way of establishing your balance again.

I don't like teaching because it's so repetitive, especially the beginning of class, which is always more or less the same and has to be carefully done. It's tedious. But I know it's necessary for dancers to keep working on technique. At least in our work it is, because the work is difficult. It's not enough to study a technique until you arrive at the point where you're skilled. I think many people stop there and think that's adequate. I always thought of that as the beginning; you have to go further and, as John Cage once said, make a few mistakes, so it's human and not simply rote.

My work always comes from the same source—from movement. It doesn't necessarily come from an outside idea, though the source can be something small or large that I've seen, often birds or other animals. The seeing then can provoke the imagining. For example, I might see a person walking in a way that I decide is odd. I don't want to know *what* caused it but *how* it was done. So then I often take it back to the studio and try to remember it physically, try to find out in my own body what it was. It's usually something that is outside of my own physical experience. It may be simply that somebody has a bad leg (which, unfortunately, *is* in my physical experience) or it may be a shape or rhythm that strikes me about the movement. I think anything can feed you, depending on the way you look at it or listen to it.

What really made me think about space and begin to think about ways to use it was Einstein's statement that there are no fixed points in space. Everything in the universe is moving all the time. His statement gave rise to the idea that in choreographing a dance you didn't have to have some sort of central point being more important than any other. You could have something happen at any point on the stage and it would be just as important as something happening somewhere else. You could have several groups in the space at the same time. I thought immediately that it's a remarkable way to think about the stage. So I applied it.

The solution to a practical theater problem sometimes has led me in new directions. In 1964 the first "Event" happened because the company was performing in a space where there wasn't a stage. Instead of our showing complete dances, I decided to put together a piece using excerpts from the repertory that the company was doing on that tour. We called it *Museum Event #1*. And we discovered that this worked well and was a way to use unconventional spaces—whether other museums, as we did later in that tour, or the Piazza San Marco in Venice, or Grand Central Station.

My process has changed over the years. I'd say it has been enhanced. When I began working with John Cage in the 1940s we soon separated the music and the dance. He would compose a piece of music and I would choreograph a dance of the same duration, but we didn't have to know anything more about what the other was doing. That independence immediately provoked a whole different way of working physically. The dancers had to learn how to be consistent in the timing of their movement so that no matter what they heard in performance, the dance would take the same amount of time to perform. I began to use a stopwatch in rehearsal. This way of working was difficult but, at the same time, it was unbelievably interesting and has remained that way. The dance was freed to have its own rhythms, as was the music. Steps could be organized independently of the sound. In one particular moment in one of those early pieces, even before we had completely separated the music and the dance, I did a strong movement and then John made a strong sound, but separately. That was a moment for me when I saw that if the two had been planned to happen together, it would have been conventional and unsurprising. But this way it was different. The independence allowed for a sense of freedom. The dancers weren't dependent on the music. John didn't want the music to dictate to the dance or the dance to dictate to the music, which was the situation that had existed before. The separation was his idea.

Then the use of chance operations opened out my way of working. The body tends to be habitual. The use of chance allowed us to find new ways to move and to put movements together that would not otherwise have been available to us. It revealed possibilities that were always there except that my mind hadn't seen them. A chance system can be used to determine the sequence of phrases and where in space they will occur. It can determine the timing and rhythm of particular movements or which dancers will do a given phrase. I sometimes throw dice using the *I Ching,* the Chinese *Book of Changes.* Since there are sixty-four hexagrams in the *I Ching,* I throw eight-sided dice, which allows me to generate eight-times-eight decisions. If I use chance to come up with a sequence of movements, I might consider the outcome and think, "Well, is that possible?" Of course, even if I devise something by chance operations I then have to work it out by exploring movement physically—on myself or more often lately it may be on the dancers. We try it out and maybe it isn't possible, but some other possibilities come up. In using chance operations the mind is enriched.

By the early 1970s I was beginning to work with video. I had never before had anything to do with a camera. With Charles Atlas, then with Elliot Caplan, the company made several dance films—or film dances—or whatever they want to call them. Originally I made these dances entirely for camera even though later I changed some of them into stage works. I saw immediately when I looked through the camera that there is a basic difference in the way the space is perceived. On the stage we see the space as wide to narrow. In the camera it's the other way; we see narrow to wide. It's a technical difference. And I found it stimulating. And, like everything else, difficult.

While we were making work for television I realized that when people are watching television, they can always turn the channel. If you simply repeat the movement, they're going to see what's on someplace else. But fortunately with the camera you have recourse to possibilities that are not available on the stage. You can do one repeat and then catch the movement from the other side, and so on. You can see things in such detail. And the technology! Even in my limited involvement, it has *jumped.*

With dance computers, the technology can take you even further. I have been working with the LifeForms program since the early nineties. Using LifeForms, if you put a computer-generated figure into one position and then into another, the program does the transition from one to the other. You can first make the phrases on the computer, then teach them to the dancers. The resulting movements may be more peculiar than a body would tend to do. That interests me. Before I meet with the dancers these days I start by making movement, which I may have worked out to some extent on the computer. Then I bring it to the dancers and work together with them within my capacity but also with their gifts. I show them first what the legs are doing. Then I add the torso and finally the arms, so they all know all the material. But then I can break it down into who does what, when they do it, and where. That's when I begin to see what we have and change it if need be. The changes may be for practical reasons or because I now see other possibilities. I use the computer as a tool. Like chance or the camera or the other tools I've used, it can open my eye to other ways of seeing or of making dances. It's not simply to do a trick. These are not tricks to me, but real things that are *in life*.

Possibilities came up through working with other artists, particularly Cage of course, but other composers as well, and certainly with visual artists. Even though we don't work the same way, I have found their ideas so interesting. In the early years of our working, dancers generally didn't know anything about the visual world. I remember one time the artist Bob Rauschenberg did some lighting for us at a summer school and the producers there thought he was crazy because he didn't know anything about what lights could do. Then I told them to just let him do what he wants; I had to fight to get them to do that. And what he did was marvelous. The next summer he began to be known. Then they wanted him to do a poster!

Rauschenberg and I still sometimes work together. He made the stunning décor a couple of years ago for *Interscape*. Although he lives in Florida, he came to New York and looked at the dance when it was partially done. He wanted to know all the dancers' names and had Polaroid pictures taken of each one. He took the photos back to Florida and made the costumes particularly for each of the dancers. What he did was beautiful. That kind of collaboration I enjoy very much.

At the beginning of each piece I usually have some idea about its length. After all, the composer needs to know. One of my recent pieces, I think it was *BIPED*, was forty-five minutes long because the commission stipulated that length. I thought, "Okay, that's fine. We'll deal with that length."

Rehearsal of *Second Hand* by Merce Cunningham, with John Cage at piano (photo James Klosty)

Field and Figures by Merce Cunningham (photo Tom Brazil)

Often the composer will want to know something else as well. Cage always wanted to know what my structure was, if I had one. I often did have some sense of the time structure. Then he'd make a *different* one for the music. It's not more detailed than that when we start, although the composer can always ask questions or come and look.

Fortunately, dance has been what's interested me all my life. So whether I am faced with incapacities or not, it still absorbs me. When years ago the press was so bitter against us, I remember once thinking I should read the reviews. I read some of that stuff and then just quit looking at it. And since then I never read it; I don't care. Maybe their critiques are right in the sense that I'm not using these possible ideas very well. But it's what *interests* me. That's stronger than anything they could say or write. I don't mean it was easy to ignore a negative response. It's hard to present dances and see everybody turn away.

Sometimes, because of deadlines, we have to present a piece when, for me, it isn't quite finished. I have limited choreographic time and I always know what the deadline is. But because of the complexity of the way I work—which continues to get more complex—it takes a long time. This is not so much because of the dancers, who are quite quick, but with *my* figuring it out. After we present it I continue working on it until I consider it finished. That point might occur a month or so after the opening. That's fine. When I get to the end of a piece I'm usually relieved, in a way. Then we put it aside and don't think about it for a while—unless we have to rehearse it for an upcoming performance.

Nowadays we are more likely to keep only recent dances in repertory. But lately there have been requests for us to bring back *Summerspace*, originally done in 1958, and *RainForest*, from 1968. We're also bringing back *Native Green*, a short dance from 1985. I don't mind reviving pieces, except that sometimes the old notes aren't sufficient. Robert Swinston, who helps me, is marvelous at it. If we're going to do an old work, then I want it done as clearly and as accurately as we can do it, and not just flub it off, even knowing that with different dancers it's going to be different.

Old work may also be revived for another company. Carolyn Brown, who was in the original *Summerspace*, set it for the ballet in Zurich. My dance *CRWDSPCR*, which is a fairly recent work, was done by the Swedish Ballet in Stockholm several years ago. When the Swedish dancers first looked at tapes of the dance they said, "We could never dance that fast!" But Petter Jacobsson, who runs the Swedish company, said he thinks it went well and they were very happy.

In preparation for the dance *Ocean*, John Cage thought about the music and had the idea that the dancing would be in the center of a circle around which the audience would sit. And around the audience would be the musicians, who would create an ocean of sound. I thought it was a very beautiful idea. When he died in 1992 we had to give it all up. But it came back not long after John's death. Andrew Culver made *Ocean* possible since he had previously entered Cage's musical ideas for this piece into the computer. David Tudor helped too. He contributed by composing electronically using underwater sounds.

We were offered a venue in Brussels that was a circle. So I thought, "Okay, we'll go ahead." And so it was agreed. I made the choreography—ninety minutes without a break. I remember that in our studio I marked a forty-foot diameter circle so that I'd have the spatial parameter. I worked out phrases and I got into the space and started doing one phrase in the circle and suddenly I thought, "Which way do I face?" And then I decided to use chance all the way through, for every single thing. You take a step; then by a chance process you determine which way you face. It brought in new movements and a wholly different idea about how to carry on. The open use of space was pushed to the absolute limit and working this way was very difficult for all of us. But the dancers were wonderful. In the end I think it turned out to be a really interesting piece. We did it in circles in nine different venues, including Japan. And each time I thought, "Well, it was difficult to do, terribly difficult to keep up, and very hard to find places to do it. But it was still worth it."

New York City
May 10, 2001

Supplemented by interview with David Vaughan
New York City
March 28, 2003

2
Anna Halprin (b. 1920)

Anna Halprin was raised in rural Winnetka, Illinois, a suburb of Chicago, where one of her cherished memories was seeing her Hasidic grandfather dancing in the synagogue. At the University of Wisconsin at Madison she studied dance with Margaret H'Doubler, who taught an objective, anatomical exploration of the body's movements and encouraged individual creativity. After graduating, Halprin joined her husband, landscape architect Lawrence Halprin, in Cambridge, Massachusetts, where she met Bauhaus artists and was influenced by their work. In 1948 Halprin and her husband moved to Marin County near San Francisco, where they have lived ever since. The outdoor dance deck adjacent to her home has been the site of classes, workshops, and performances by Halprin and other dancers, composers, and artists.

Halprin is a spirited explorer who has ventured into many realms, always with the goal of integrating the artistic and the personal, the individual and the community. She founded the San Francisco Dancers' Workshop in 1959 and used improvisational methods to explore real-life issues: In 1969 she brought together two workshop groups, one black and one white, to explore and overcome their racial tensions. In the late sixties she worked with her husband to develop the RSVP Cycles, a method used to map out dances through a combination of visual and verbal instructions. Dances taught by this method don't depend on set choreography and can be easily communicated to any group of participants. Around the same time, Halprin created a series of *Myths* in which audience members were given instructions to follow and thus became cocreators and performers. After surviving cancer, she ran workshops especially for people facing life-threatening illnesses such as

AIDS and cancer, integrating their life experiences into their performances. Her researches have continued with the Tamalpa Institute, cofounded with her daughter Daria Halprin-Khalighi in 1978, and the Sea Ranch, where other artists come to experiment with her. Now in her eighties, Anna Halprin continues to make new work and to perform.

Anna Halprin is the author of *Movement Rituals, Moving Toward Life: Five Decades of Transformational Dance,* and *Dance as a Healing Art.* She has received the Samuel Scripps American Dance Festival's Award for Lifetime Achievement in Modern Dance, the American Dance Guild Award, and choreography fellowships from the John Simon Guggenheim Foundation and the National Endowment for the Arts. The University of Wisconsin granted her an honorary Doctor of Fine Arts degree.

* * *

Anna Halprin in *Memories from My Closet* (photo Julie Lemberger)

Anna Halprin

When I became disaffected from modern dance in my twenties it was because, despite modern dance's original urge to break away from ballet, I felt that there was essentially no difference between what modern dancers were doing and what ballet had always done. Some modern dances, like Doris Humphrey's *Chacon*, were purely abstract and followed the structure of music. Martha Graham made works that represented mythological stories. They were wonderful dances, fresh and with a spirit of America about them. But, like in ballet, everybody was trained to look alike, except it was based on an idiosyncratic approach to art, on somebody's personal style.

I began to question the creative process behind this kind of dance. It seemed there must be another way to generate creativity in oneself as well as in the people that you work with. It was about 1955, ten years after I came to Marin County, when I started searching. I didn't know where to begin. So I started with improvisation, setting up simple structures like asking my dancers to work with imagined forces of attraction and repulsion. I also made drawings of floor patterns and we would walk the floor patterns and see what would happen. Everything was a little bit out of control, which appealed to me. The improvisations certainly instigated new materials that I never would have thought of, that I couldn't have preconceived. This procedure interested me for maybe seven or eight years.

Then I began to notice that people were tending to repeat themselves, as if regurgitating what they already knew. So this approach too had lost its excitement. It had become so subjective that it was no longer generating new ideas. Again I wanted to find new criteria on which to base my dances. I had to consider: When is dance just self-expression that might be a cathartic experience for the person doing it and where does art come in? How do you set up a value system? This new set of questions began to drive me to investigate other ideas. I began thinking, "Well, maybe the thing to do is to work with some basic principles of movement, with space, time, and force. At least that would provide some limits." To start, we worked with "studies in space." Then there were "studies in force" and "studies in time." These explorations established underlying structures. You knew what you were doing and you knew why you were doing it.

This was fine for a while but then again I began to feel it wasn't enough. Once more I looked for something else. And that "something else" was experimenting with the *context* of these improvisations or studies. Why do these studies always have to be done in the studio? What would happen if you went outside and did them in different environments? How would that affect what you were doing? After all, we don't live our lives in a studio. We live our lives on the street, or in an office, or in the woods. So I began to explore environments where dance could take place, going to the beach and to bus stops and to grocery stores. Everywhere.

At the beach we found whole new elements to relate to—the sound of the ocean, the impact of the waves, the feeling of the sand. This led me to explore the tasks you could do in specific places. On the beach you could dig in the sand. You could carry logs from here to there. In the city you could go shopping. Tasks in found environments began to intrigue me. This approach would generate creativity and new material. In doing task-oriented movement we were looking at it from the outside as well as from the inside, with an eye to also being able to perform it. This exploration culminated in 1976 in *City Dance*, where we passed through all of San Francisco during the performance.

I was constantly looking to redefine and reinvent dance. I wanted to start from zero and build a whole new perspective. I didn't want dance to come out of one person's mind because one person's mind is too limited, and I didn't want the dancer to be an object of the choreographer's manipulations. I wanted the dancer to relate to what's real in life. For example, there is the core issue: You're not the center of the universe; you're just a part of it. So how do you deal with your relationship to all that isn't you? I kept probing. One thing just kept leading to another. Along the way, of course, I was creating dances within the context of each new procedure.

For twelve years in the late sixties and the seventies I was able to maintain a company because I was being supported by Expansion Arts. Having my own company gave me the opportunity to create and perform new pieces, but eventually it became too limiting. It became so much a business. I spent too much time trying to raise money and trying to keep the company together. I just couldn't do that and live a life. It was interfering with my process of discovery. And when we went on tour and did pieces like *Parades and Changes* and introduced nudity, then all of a sudden I was defined by that work. When I was already off to something else, people still asked, "But why aren't you doing *Parades and Changes?*" I felt trapped. For me to maintain creativity, I have to find new forms to reach out to people. Having a company and touring is one form. After having done that for at least twelve years, it didn't seem like that was the most conducive form for generating creativity any more. It didn't allow me the time to experiment. It didn't allow me the time to make mistakes or to fail. I didn't want to always be judged by critics.

Creating dances in cooperation with other people came to a head when I became interested in the multiracial context of dance in the late sixties. I said to myself, "Well, I'm a white Jewish person, so what I do is going to come out of that cultural milieu. What about African-Americans? What about Asians? What about American Indians? What do they have to do with this point of view about dance? Why should it be just this one point of view?" So I formed a multiracial company. It was really exciting. And the moment I did that I realized that there were so many differences for us to confront. How could we respect, enhance, and encourage the diversity and at the same time find our commonalities as human beings? Right away I encountered some problems. Simple, dumb misunderstandings like this: My hair tends to be frizzy and somebody from the black group came and said, "Oh sister, your hair's bad!" And I thought she meant it was awful. But she meant it was good! Now that's silly, but if you take that kind of communication and enlarge it and multiply it, it can get very serious.

About that same time I was talking to my husband Larry, who is an architect, about how to communicate through the differences I was encountering. He was interested at that time in "scoring," which was a way for him to communicate his ideas to other people through a visual representation of a plan. We developed what was known as the RSVP Cycles, which demystified the creative process through the use of scores. The letters in RSVP stand for Resources, Scores, Valuaction, and Performance, all part of the scoring process. As I use it in my work, a score is a way to map out activities with people over time in space to create a product. A five-year-old can work within a score. But before you create a score you have to collect all kinds of resources. You don't want to limit yourself to preconceived ideas of what you want to do without having experimented and explored a whole range of possibilities. Anything goes, just put it all on the table. That part of the process is called "resources." But how do you use those resources toward making a score? You need an intention. For example, an intention in response to the fire that happened in Oakland might be to give people a ritual where they can communicate their feelings of loss and despair.

You perform the score and then, to find out whether that score works, you have a "valuaction." Unlike an "evaluation," which is analytical and intellectual and doesn't incorporate the experiential aspect, a valuaction is based on experience. I got hooked into this with John Dewey and Alfred North Whitehead years and years ago. John Dewey wrote a book called *Art as Experience* and Margaret H'Doubler, my teacher at University of Wisconsin, wrote *Dance as an Art Experience*. The emphasis is on the experience. I wanted to get away from evaluation that is merely abstract. When someone says, "I think you should do this and I think you should do that," it drives me crazy, because it's judgmental. And if there's anything that will kill creativity, it's judgmental attitudes. They make you afraid to try anything because maybe it won't be right.

Although we didn't start out asking how to share creativity and demystify it so everybody is empowered to participate, it nevertheless suddenly was so clear. Everybody can interpret a score. Everybody can say, "Hey, I like this resource"; or, "Before I do this performance, I want to know what the score is because I don't want to be manipulated"; or, "I don't want to get involved in something that I don't feel committed to." Scoring covered so many problem areas. One advantage was that you could see the whole piece mapped out from beginning to end. People could look at it and maybe valuact it even before they did it. Someone could say, "I don't think this is going to work here because it seems not to be supporting the intention. Let's go back and make some more resources."

You can valuact the resources. You can valuact the score. You can valuact the performance. But you have to be careful in this process to distinguish whether you're valuacting the performance or the score because sometimes a performer will deviate from the score, so you can't say that the score isn't any good. You say, "Hey, you didn't do the score, so therefore I don't know whether the score worked or it didn't." You need to do the score first. Then we can tell whether it was your performance that needed to be changed—or recycled, as we say—or whether it's the score that needed to be recycled.

Scores can range from open, allowing the performers to make many choices in their actions, to closed, in which one's activities are predetermined. The avant-garde composer John Cage could use open scores when David Tudor performed his work because David was such a good performer and artist. He could bring to life the simplest activity, even dropping pebbles on a page and picking them up. I use open scores when I am working with people who are mature artists because I want them to use their skills. If I'm working with untrained people with whom I have ten minutes to say, "Here's the score, now do it," I have to use a closed score.

My 1987 *Planetary Dance* is a closed score. That's why it's been able to go all over the world and be done by thousands and thousands of people—in Russia, in Germany, in Spain, in thirty-six different countries. The score is very simple but it's also beautiful to look at. It tells people to stay together on a given pulse and to run. Of course, a closed score may tell you *what* to do but it doesn't necessarily tell you *how* to do it. There are a hundred ways that one can stay on the beat and run. But the score makes it visually clear what the action is. And because it's a closed score, it can be sent anywhere and people can tell exactly what to do just by looking at it. That's what I love about scoring.

When we lead the *Planetary Dance*, we show the score to the group and tell them, "The musicians are in the center. The dance starts with kneeling in the four directions. You can give the directions a particular meaning if you want. Next you run clockwise. The lines on the score show the direction of the run. Easy, right? And then you're going to run the other way on a circle inside the first—because you can't run in the same direction without eventually losing your alertness. You get woozy. In the meantime more people keep joining. So now you have two groups running. You may even have a third group so that the people who get tired from the running but don't want to stop dancing can face one of the four directions and just be still." Every time I do this dance—and I've been doing it now as a ritual for twenty-four years—we do it a little differently. We found that when we brought in teenagers, they needed an outer circle where they could run with more vigor. And if we had older people who could do a little bit of jogging, we had a middle run. So it dealt with generational differences. It's simple but it builds according to people's needs. After maybe an hour of running and calling out their dedications, finally everybody comes and kneels again, rests, and says a prayer.

The aspect of the score that's open and that makes it so human is that the performers dedicate the dance to someone, either to an ancestor, or to someone who needs their help, or to the future—which means to the children. By doing this, the performers have so much invested in the score that it comes to life in a way that is deeply touching. I had a man from Ghana who did this score and dedicated it to his brother who had been killed ten years earlier. He had never mentioned his brother's name in all that time. And so when I said you can dance for an ancestor or someone you feel you want to communicate with, he said, "I dance for John." It was the first time he had called his name in ten years! As you can imagine, his run had a determination, a depth, a spirit that was like a blazing light. In the valuation after the dance, he thanked everybody in the group for supporting him. He felt that he had embodied John in the dance and that he could now go back any time he wanted to and be with John. He felt resolved. If people have a personal reason in their life to dance, it's going to have a heart, a meaning that is so profound that, even just witnessing it, you feel it too. Even though the *Planetary Dance* is a very closed score, that doesn't mean it can't have tremendous meaning. Within a closed score wonderful things can happen because we're not asking the performers to think about steps or about specific movements, just about actions and tasks everybody can do. The score for *Planetary Dance* allowed each of them to find their own meaning.

As for aesthetics, if the performance of a score were meant to be witnessed by other people, then, sure, I'd want it to be visually coherent. If I'm performing at Zellerbach Auditorium on the University of California campus or in some other formal situation, I'll spend a year on a piece to bring it to absolute perfection. I'm an artist and I'll use artistic skills. But it doesn't mean that everything that I do is going to be artistically the greatest dance in the world.

I don't believe in setting up a single standard for pieces with different goals. The question "Is it art?" is valid. But why limit yourself? Why not be able to use art for various purposes: to develop a sense of community, or to give people the opportunity to work with children, with adolescents, or with old people? Participatory dances that have no audience are based on art because an experience that enables people to find the full depth of their humanness *is* an art experience. So I would say, yes, the *Planetary Dance* was a beautiful art experience. We used movement that was shaped by each person's individual expression and experience. The mandala configuration used the space symbolically and mythologically. The rhythm was powerful because it became like one voice. Artistically for that intention it was fine.

Scores themselves produce ideas that you would never have thought of. "Oh, my God, look what happens when you put this together with that and that together with this! Wow! I could never have preconceived that combination." When I arrived at scoring, I had finally found a process that has discipline, that's accountable, and that really communicates with everybody at every level. It also communicates among collaborators. You can work with a musician, a sculptor, an actor, a dancer, with anybody using the scoring method. Musicians work with scores all the time. I know when we did *Parades and Changes* in the mid-sixties, the composer Morton Subotnick developed the most wonderful scores. They were all in the form of cards, and every activity had a card. The sculptor had his own; so did the dancers. The lighting person had different cards for different kinds of lighting and the musician had different cards for various episodes of music. Every time we went into a different theater we would look at the space, the context, and we would study what the space was saying. Then we'd rearrange the cards. I'd put a new movement card here with this musician's card. Every night it would be a different dance—but we weren't improvising.

It was such a brilliant score that I began to adapt it for many uses. I have a big chart on which there are wheels that you can turn. Each wheel has different elements in it, and when you turn them they line up differently. Anybody can turn the wheels to new positions and say, "Okay, this is what the score's going to be." You don't know until you do it what it's going to produce. I think this process stimulates creativity. When I'm developing scores with others, it isn't enough that it satisfies my personal goals. One of my personal criteria for the success of a score is that it generates creativity in the performers.

When Larry and I were first studying scoring with the lab group we were running, we were looking for ways of developing simple scores. But then we became interested in making them more and more complex and in being able to shift so that the elements in a given score were not all closed or all open. As the scores got more complex we had to figure out how best to present them. We learned how to express ideas graphically rather than verbally. When you speak, you convey one idea at a time. But when you present ideas graphically, they can all be seen holistically. You can show that *this* is going on at the same time as *that*.

In scoring, you have four elements: *activity* over *time* and *space*, with *people*. The levels of openness of each element can be set from one to ten; ten is closed. Every activity in the *Planetary Dance* is closed except the one aspect of the performers' calling out their personal commitments. But in another piece, space can be set at five so it's partly closed, partly open, while the rhythm or the time element might be set at ten, completely closed. You can have activity very open but the use of people very closed. It's wonderful how you can manipulate these elements. In the scoring process you start out with a score that you've taken to a certain level. Then you get input from the performers and you "recycle" the score. There's always more to consider. That's what I did recently with *Intensive Care*. We would make a score, then open it up to improvisation. Then we'd close it. It's an iterative process. I like to reach a point of having a definitive score, but then open it up again. We might completely open up the use of space. Try this, try that. Then close it up again. Then when it's closed, if we feel that something's not working, we open it up again. So it's like an accordion, constantly opening up and then closing, now with new material. That way it keeps expanding its possibilities. I haven't done *Intensive Care* for a year and we've been invited to go to Paris to do it. I've looked at the videotapes and said to myself, "Oh, God, why didn't I think to do this other option?" That process repeats itself over and over again. I never seem to be finished with anything. Nothing ever seems to be perfect.

I'm interested in relating to the audience, but there are many ways to do it. I did my eightieth retrospective a few years ago in a proscenium theater. One of the dances I performed was called *Memories from My Closet*. In making the piece, I took different articles of clothing out of my closet that evoked memories and also became my costumes. A pair of beautiful old silk pajamas led me to talk about my grandfather, who was a tailor. I talked about aging. I shared my personal stories. "When I was five years old, I used to dance for the fun of it. Then when I was a teenager, I danced to rebel." I verbalized all the way through that dance. "Then when I was half of a hundred I danced to heal. And when I'm 110, I will dance the way things really are." Using narration to create an intimate biography was my way of bringing the audience into my personal life.

Early in my career, when I began to move out beyond the proscenium arch and into the audience space, I was naïve and innocent because, of course, when audience members attend the theater, they follow a tacit score. It tells you where to walk and what seat to take. It tells you to shut up when the lights go down. It tells you that when the lights go up you can get up and go pee or get something to eat or talk to your friends. It tells you that the performance is going to start when the curtain opens and that it's going to end when the curtain closes. When I started saying to myself, "Well, I don't have to stay here, I can go out into the aisles; I can go overhead; I can come up from the pit," I didn't realize that I was treading on somebody else's territory. And this was threatening. In Italy, during *Esposizione* in 1963, somebody walked down the aisle and stood in front and said, "For this, Columbus had to discover America?" Somebody else threw shoes at us. We were getting violent responses. I was floored. But finally I realized, of course, I'm in your territory, with no explanation. I just bulldozed right in.

So when I came back from tour—this was the late sixties—I started creating scores for the audiences to do, which I called *Myths*. The audience would arrive and discover that they were also performers. We used two rooms. In one room I would brief them on what they were going to do. Then they would go into the other room where an environment would have been set up, where they would do the score. But we found that, on their own initiative, they would break the score and create one of their own. I did ten of these and I was astonished at what they would create—without talking to each other. How easily they started out doing my form, but how easily they broke it. It was as though the score got them going and initiated some creativity. But they'd have their own sense about where they wanted to take it, and they would just take it there. It was so exciting. I marveled, "Wow, look at what they're doing! I never could have thought of that when I did this score!"

Rehearsal of *Esposizione* by Anna Halprin (photographer unknown)

Anna Halprin in *Apartment 6* (photographer unknown)

So I spent a year working on the myths and learning from the alterations audiences made to the score, learning something about how they created their own myths. They would sometimes have a hero, one person who would be lifted up in the air or become the center of attraction. This was just remarkable to me.

So those discoveries, combined with my having cancer in 1972 and asking myself a whole bunch of new questions—"Who am I dancing for? Why am I dancing? What am I dancing about? What difference does it make in one's life?"—led me to focus on rituals. The purpose of a ritual was to take a situation and make it better, to bring about change. How could dance transform? That's what eventually got me going in healing and working with people with life-threatening situations. I began to think about the meaning of dance and how it plugged into people's lives. I came up with this idea: "As your art expression expands, your life experience deepens; and as your life experience deepens, your art expression expands." The two are interactive. I began to work seriously with making dances that had content, that had to do with transforming people's lives. Otherwise, why do it? Who cares? Who needs another dance performance? That was my personal link and it meant a major shift.

Our group's work with the reality of life and death changed our relationship to the audience. We brought our individual contacts with death and dying to our performances. I had been working with people with cancer who were dying. I've survived cancer, but I'm old and I know that death is something for me to prepare for. One of the performers works in hospice and is close to people dying every day. When we did the piece *Intensive Care*, somebody performing in the group was facing his impending death. This was put in the program notes, which revealed the immediacy and was another way of bringing the audience in. We weren't talking about death in general. We were talking about our personal experience with death. The man who was dying had been told that he would probably live for about a month, but he lived for a year to perform that dance. And that dance was a rehearsal for his death. Later, as he was dying, he told me the score he wanted us to do at the beach for his memorial.

With my new piece, *Seasons*, we take the audience on a voyage. We're planning to do one installment in the summer, one in the fall, one in the winter, and one in the spring. In a couple of weeks for part 1/*Summer,* the audience comes to our place in the woods. They walk in, and the stairs become their viewing platform. They see a grove of trees in which seven pods—people hanging in mesh casings—are hanging from the trees. The audience is almost close enough to touch these pods. It's so evocative. Next they're looking at an installation where the men are performing right above them. Again, it's a direct sensorial experience. Then the audience does a blindfold walk, so suddenly they're the performers, not the viewers. They experience it. Then they go through pathways where they see more installations being made. In one, there's a group of people collecting sticks. A little bit further the audience sees people wrapped around trees, becoming extensions of the trees. They're in nature, looking at nature from a totally new perspective. It's another way of being.

The theme of *Summer* is emergence. All the episodes have to do with being in darkness and coming into light. At the end the audience sees feathers dropping from the heights of a redwood tree. They look up and there's a figure flying forty feet in the air in a birdlike image as if he's become complete emergence and complete light. As he slowly drifts down it becomes evident why some of the dancers had been collecting sticks for an hour: They've been making a nest. The bird/man is received in the nest. As the audience walks from one event to another, there's always a kind of musical interlude, so they're walking in relation to the rhythm. They too are dancing as they move from one site to another.

When they finally come back, we do a food ritual together, which is done according to a score. One third of the people are making the environment, another group is organizing the food that everyone has brought, and the third group is working on the presentation of the meal. So they've created their own ritual and then we all eat together.

In the last part we work with nighttime and make a labyrinth out of light ropes—plastic strips lined with small lights. This section has to do with the feeling of going into one's personal darkness. It's intensely painful to think about what's happening in the world now, how we've been affected by what's happening, and the wars that have been maiming people. Then the dancers come into the center of the labyrinth and there's a section we call "contact contour." They connect with each other and then they go out and find some hope in nature. People are familiar with a labyrinth but they've never seen one approached as a dance. I'm still exploring how to incorporate the audience. I'll give out paper and pencil so that as they're watching the labyrinth dance, which takes about forty minutes, they're writing their responses to the images or they're drawing what they see. They're active. I'm still experimenting with that.

We'll do a big valuaction after *Summer* to find out how to "recycle" it and make it artistically clearer in its intent and how to better integrate the audience from the moment they arrive. When you come into an environment like this there's no preestablished score for the audience. Where do you sit? What do you look at? When is there intermission? It's a wonderful opportunity to redefine an audience. It may be a dud. We'll see.

I have a group of people who do research with me every year up at the Sea Ranch on the Pacific coast. We work intensely. Kei Takei, who trained with me, is coming back. Also the Butoh dancer Kan Katsura, the dancer Alain Buffant from France, and Eeo Stubblefield, who's been working together with me for thirty years. This group experiments together. The new piece, *Summer*, is the first time we've taken experimentation from the Sea Ranch and turned it into a performance for other people to see. We're primarily a research group. I identify a lot with the Polish theater innovator Jerzy Grotowski, who had a research group in France. He did performances with only ten people in the audience because he was interested in creativity rather than having a company that would spend a year performing the same thing. I try now to do a little of both. I bring the work to the public, which challenges me to bring it up to the highest artistic standard I can go for. I also want to be able to reach out to different communities because that, in turn, expands my vision.

Working with real situations has become my focus. I had some of the most touching and meaningful experiences working with very old people at the nursing home where my mother was living and seeing the joy that the experience brought them. I also work with a group of people with AIDS and HIV. A young man came into class one night and said he was "going home" and everybody knew he was going home to die. When he left, there was complete silence. Everyone was paralyzed. So I set up a movement situation where they could touch each other, which led to a dance that was called *Carry Me Home*. That dance was about: When I die, I will go home. But it asked the question, What is home? The group created a dance that was performed in front of an audience. They got such a wonderful ovation, which lifted their spirits and made them feel they had accomplished something.

Again, scoring was the methodology for making this dance. I had found in my own experience with cancer that the healing process had a structure and progression to it. For twenty years I worked with people with life-threatening illness and I noticed that they go through the same five stages I experienced. So when I developed scores for this group, I developed them on the basis of those five stages: The first score was identification, the second one was confrontation, the third was release, the fourth was change, the fifth was integration and transformation.

I used to be discouraged that people in the dance world would just slough this work off as therapy and say that I wasn't doing art. But I could see how important this work was and how limiting it is to say that there's only one way to dance. Like the ancient Persian poet Rumi says, "There's a hundred ways to kiss the floor." There's also a hundred ways to dance. Who am I or who are you to judge what is right and wrong? It used to make me sad, but then I would just teach harder and get more people to appreciate all the different applications that dance could have. In archaic times people danced to have courage to meet a battle or to heal a person in the community or to inaugurate a young person into adulthood. Dance could once again become an integral part of people's lives. I am driven by a desire to see all the different ways dance can be meaningful to us. I'm looking forward to what's going to happen next. I have no idea what it will be.

Kentfield, California
June 5, 2003

3

David Gordon (b. 1936)

David Gordon grew up in New York City and studied fine arts at Brooklyn College. Without having formally studied dance, he was drawn into performing and first danced professionally with James Waring in the late 1950s. He was one of the members of Robert Ellis Dunn's classes in the early 1960s that led choreographers toward the pursuit of unprescribed methods and materials and resulted in the Judson Dance Theater. Gordon went on to work with Yvonne Rainer in her *Continuous Project-Altered Daily*, in which she and her dancers explored the interplay between choreography, rehearsal, and performance. During 1970–76 Gordon was a member of Grand Union, an improvisational performing group that spun off from Rainer's work, in which his talent for impromptu verbal wit contributed to the group's complexly theatrical, multileveled performances.

Seeing Gordon's combination of dance, text, and theater, audiences are often unsure what is ad lib and what is set, what is autobiography and what is artifice. Visual and verbal *double entendres* create multiple layers of uncertain meaning. This perplexity is further compounded by the fact that his wife Valda Setterfield is one of his performers, sometimes in the role of his wife. He is a master at developing a small amount of material in close detail. He has used doors, frames, and screens rather like dancers, choreographing them into his work in an almost mathematical permutation of locations and actions. His work is smart and funny. As Gordon put it, "My work is too funny to be taken seriously and too serious to be entertaining. I don't think what I do is clever. I think what I do is serious. I think I make seriously funny work."

David Gordon started working with a group of dancers in 1971 and formally organized his Pick Up Performance Company in 1978. He has had commissions for directing and/or choreographing from Danspace Project, Brooklyn Academy of Music, American Ballet Theatre, the Guthrie Theater, the Dance Theater of Harlem, the White Oak Dance Project, Mark Taper Forum, Serious Fun at Lincoln Center, and the Spoleto Festival USA, among others, and from PBS's *Great Performances*, ALIVE TV, and the BBC. His awards include two John Simon Guggenheim Fellowships, three New York Dance and Performance (Bessie) Awards, two Obies, and two National Residency Fellowships from the Pew Charitable Trust in both theater and dance.

* * *

David Gordon in *My Folks* (photo Chris Ha)

David Gordon

In the mid-fifties I was a fine arts major at Brooklyn College and was interested in an attractive young woman who was in the modern dance club. One day I walked her to the club and the next thing I knew I was *in* the club and, though I had no training, I was immediately put into a dance. (Guys were hard to find and it turned out I had presence and could stand on one leg.) Next I met Jimmy Waring who invited me to audition for his company and, when I got there, it wasn't an audition, it was a rehearsal and I was in the company. Then Valda Setterfield emigrated from England to America and David Vaughan took her to meet Jimmy. She walked into a rehearsal that I was in and Jimmy said, "I should make a duet for the two of you," and he did, and Valda and I began to dance together.

I think if I hadn't met Valda, I probably would have quit dancing. Instead, I married her and, having married a real dancer, I gained the knowledge of, and respect for, her qualities of discipline, ambition and determination—none of which I had. I stayed married and I stayed dancing. But I couldn't make a living doing this kind of dancing and, since I was a would-be-upwardly-mobile-lower-class kid who wanted to have nice things and to live well, for the first twenty years of our marriage I also did a lot of freelance design jobs and window displays (and got pretty well known). This work supported my dancing and supported Valda's dancing with Merce Cunningham.

I was one of the people involved in Robert Ellis Dunn and Judith Dunn's dance composition classes in the early 1960s. (Valda was pregnant at the time and showed up occasionally.) The work produced for that class led to a series of unpredictable dance/art/theater concerts at the Judson Memorial Church on Washington Square. For a while after the Judson Dance Theater performances I continued to make solos but, after Valda gave birth, I began to make duets for us because we could rehearse quietly alone together in our living room.

In 1966 Steve Paxton and Yvonne Rainer were planning a concert, again at the Judson, and asked if I would share the concert with them. During that evening my new solo, *Walks and Digressions*, was mightily booed. The audience stamped their feet and came right up to me as they walked out and booed in my face. I finished the dance but I came away from that evening and sat in a corner like a whipped boy and said, "What am I doing? I am a private person and I won't let this happen to me. I'm not doing this any more. I quit." I retired from dancing. I stopped doing anything except design work—which paid.

My ego was beginning to heal when I happened to have a casual conversation with Yvonne in a social situation in which she said, "Aren't you ever going to…?" and I said, "No. But if you want me to be in your work, I think it's really interesting and I'll do that. And that way if they boo, they boo you and not me and I can live with that." So I went to work for Yvonne in *Continuous Project-Altered Daily* (which was very interesting to do). But by the time *Continuous Project* actually happened, Yvonne was sliding into some kind of democracy in which we were all going to make decisions and I didn't want that. I was saying, "Uh, oh," to myself, but I couldn't make myself leave, and around 1970, out of Yvonne's work, Grand Union emerged. We did improvisational performances, though everything I did in that first Grand Union year was Yvonne Rainer material. Everybody else was inventing stuff, but not me. I just did her *Trio A* faster, slower, in a corner, in a box, upside down, and backward. I did not want to be responsible for making new material. I was responsible for my performance of Yvonne's material and that was it.

I was the only one for whom this was an issue. The others already thought of themselves as downtown artists; I thought of myself only as a fellow who was smart and had some kind of talent. They all went to see each other's work. I would come to rehearsal and they would all be talking about art. Yvonne would say, "And what have you seen?" And I would say, "I just saw Bea Lillie in *Auntie Mame*," or, "I just saw Ginger Rogers in *Hello Dolly*." I went to see every replacement in *Hello Dolly* on Broadway. I wanted to understand what interpretation meant. I chewed on theater and television and film and literature and the things that interested me personally, none of which I thought about in relation to anything called "art." The Grand Union was made up of distinctly different sensibilities and tastes. We applied those faculties to the investigation and performance of material that was itself in flux.

I think it was Steve who suggested we do a series of performances at Claes Oldenberg's loft on East 13th Street and I agreed because they all agreed but I was still doing only *Trio A*. Then something went wrong in Steve's belly and he had to go to Saint Vincent's Hospital, where I went to visit him. In the same ward as Steve there was a very old man, with pale, waxy skin, wrapped in a sheet, sitting in a chair. The old man began to slide down in the chair. As he was sliding, he moaned and cried out, "Oh, Lord, I'm slipping. I'm slipping, Lord." When he got far enough and loud enough, somebody came in and propped him back up. I continued visiting with Steve and watching the old man, and the old man's process started again: "Oh, Lord, I'm slipping." It was poignant and comic and my idea of a theatrical event.

At the next Grand Union performance, Barbara Dilley very particularly started to follow me. This had never happened before. She was on my tail and copying my actions. Seeing her doing what I was doing, I began to try things in order to get her to do those things and I began to say, "Oh, Lord, I'm slipping." Barbara was right behind me saying, "Oh, Lord …" And I slipped and rolled, "Oh, Lord." (This was all happening on gym mats.) And now somebody else in the group was looking over and starting to pick up the movement and starting to pick up the words and now we had this trio going, slipping and rolling, "Oh, Lord, oh, Lord." I was amazed. I began hesitantly in performances after that to initiate material to see if anybody came with me. And they did. And they didn't blame me if it didn't turn into much of anything. I liked it.

Then Yvonne persuaded Trisha Brown to come and join up with us. At rehearsal one day Trisha started making up verbal material. We were all moving around the studio in some kind of parade and I picked up the verbal material and I started laughing and turned the laughing into crying. I was aware that Trisha was still doing what she had initiated but she was taking note of what I was doing.

We all agreed to do a series of performances at The Kitchen. Trisha started to work with me physically in the performance, saying, "Tell me about something or other." So I was working with Trisha and telling her about something or other and by now Trisha was on her back on the floor with her arms and legs in the air and I was lying across her hands and feet and she was balancing me in the air and saying, "Keep telling me the story." Now Nancy Green and Barbara were coming over to us and Trisha was saying, "Pay no attention to them; just keep talking to me." And Trisha somehow got up off the floor and got me on her shoulders and was ramming me into a column and saying, "Keep talking, keep talking!"

In the Grand Union it was Trisha who initially pushed for this verbal stuff, but actually I had been talking a long time before it resurfaced there. In 1962 at the Judson, in the beginning of my piece *Random Breakfast*, I walked out and talked to the audience. I went through all of modern dance history as I knew it, using everybody's signature movement. And I did a dance in Carmen Miranda drag and babbled in fake Spanish. It never occurred to me that I was breaking rules by connecting verbal theatrical material and physical movement material.

More than ten years later Michael Kirby asked me to write a piece for *The Drama Review* about what I had done. I agreed to do it in one of those moments in which I said to myself, "You always say no, say yes." I went home and started to write. I didn't know what I was doing. How would this all fit together? Eventually I called Yvonne and said, "Could I come over and talk with you? I have a pile of writing I want to show you, all right?" I went over and put all the pieces of paper on the table and said, "I think I'm just going to tell him I can't do this."

Yvonne said, "David, don't you know what you contributed?"

"Really, I don't."

"In *Random Breakfast* you improvised an entire solo. Nobody was improvising."

"Well, that wasn't really improvisation. I knew the through-line of what I was doing and I went out and played with the material."

"Yes, David, that was improvisation."

"But I can't say that about myself."

"Yes, you can say it about yourself."

So I went home and wrote the article called "It's About Time," and it got published.

During the time I was in Yvonne's work and near the beginning of the Grand Union, around 1970, Yvonne got a fellowship to go to India. She had gathered a number of young artists and art students in New York who were all in the large group sections of certain pieces of hers and she wanted to keep those people together. She asked me if I would teach them once or twice a week. "Would I make sure they all stayed together?" I was flattered and did not consider that I had nothing to teach and agreed to do it. By about the third time we met, I had taught them everything I could figure out to teach. So, over the weeks I began to invent some material that they could do together and that's what resulted in the dance that became my first piece back in business, *Sleepwalking*. It had references to what you would see those days on the streets of New York. This was before the methadone clinics opened. Addicts were standing in the streets, nodding out, and I would stand and watch. I was fascinated by the amazing off-balance that people could maintain in a half-conscious state without actually falling over. And I practiced how they did that and I taught it to Yvonne's people and that's how I began making work again.

I was still making no money dancing. I was still making money designing. Valda and I and our son Ain, who was then fourteen, were living in an inexpensive floor-through apartment in a brownstone in the village (you could do that then) when Trisha Brown found a loft building for sale and said, "You must come and live and work here." So, we bought one of the lofts (you could do that then) and I said to Valda and Ain, "We won't have Guerlain soap for a while but we'll have a space to work in. Is it okay if I take two years to see if I can make a living dancing?" I quit all my design jobs. That was twenty-seven years ago.

In the beginning years of my working with other dancers, I would go into the studio and make up the movement on my own body first and then teach it to them and make sure they did it exactly like I did. For a while I had a company with three women other than Valda and one other man. That was the first company in which it began to occur to me that they were capable of doing physical, technical dancing I had never been capable of doing and was not going to get capable of doing, and that I was not taking advantage of what they could do. I restricted them with my limitations. That seemed really crazy.

So I spent a great part of rehearsal that year apologizing to them for taking time to find movement with them rather then having it all prepared. At one point they called a meeting in which they told me they were happy to wait, it was really okay, and would I stop apologizing. And so the work began to change in response to the range of what the dancers could do.

Nowadays, Karen Graham, who has been dancing with me for about sixteen years, sometimes comes to rehearse with me alone for about a week before anyone else comes. I try things out with her. I say, "This is in my head, I can't show you in my body. But is this possible?" And she begins to make notes, so that by the time the dancers arrive, Karen is there to tell them what we're dealing with. I am listening to her and watching her show some material and I am seeing the work now filtered through her: both what has been made better by her understanding and her way of moving and what I think has been lost by her understanding and her way of moving. So I begin to correct on the bodies of the other dancers anything that I feel may have been evened out—which I am not interested in having happen.

Then, as we put it all together, each of them may have some of the same movement and presumably some of the same intention, but they don't all have the same body. I watch the various ways that everybody does the stuff. "Okay, hold it. Do you see the way she does that movement? Can you try and see what happens if you do it that way? Okay, can you hold on to what it is you're doing against what she's doing? And can *you* hold on to what it is you're doing against the two of them? Then, instead of looking like you're trying to do the same thing, can you stay out of sync with them?" I'm gathering; I'm accumulating images; I'm drawing; I'm painting and framing. I don't know yet what it all means.

When I was a kid, living the Lower East Side tenement life, my mother would say, "Go for a walk with your brother. Take your brother for a walk. Hold his hand." I would take him out and work hard to get lost so that he would get scared and so would I. I'm still trying to get lost. In making a new work, I attempt to start someplace that I haven't started before. Sometimes

I put a piece of music on the machine and I work in relation to that music. Then I pull it off and I put on another piece of music and try the same material. I do what it takes to upset the balance of knowing.

When I was designing store windows, nobody ever told me what to put in the window. I walked into the store and looked at what was new and what was not moving off the shelves. I gathered the merchandise together in the window and climbed in and began to build around myself. I taught myself early on not to have to jump out of the window, walk through the store, go out the door, step into the street, and stand in front of the window to see if the last thing I moved was okay. I taught myself to be able to visualize what it looked like out there without actually seeing it and then to check one or two times close to the end to see if everything looked the way I thought it did.

Similarly, in making physical work, as you accumulate material, you know pretty well how things might fit together. But you may add one element and think, "I don't really understand this in relation to what's already going on. I have to step out and look at this." Doing windows affected the process of working on a proscenium stage, and that process then needed reexamining for thrust stages. These are not discrete cells of information that have nothing to do with one another. They are all related.

Sometimes the variation on one's own process is dictated by working with other companies. For the Guthrie Theater I read many scripts, trying to pick one to direct and choreograph that had some meaning to me. I chose *The Firebugs* by Max Frisch, opted for a new translation, and began to work with the casting director. It was all a more sequential, linear process than I was used to. Working there, all the circumstances are well under way on the day you walk into rehearsal with the chosen cast, the chosen designer, the chosen composer.

At American Ballet Theatre, they need to know the music that you are going to use months ahead of time. They need to figure out the orchestration and the rehearsal piano reduction and the cost, of course. When I made the first ballet, *Field, Chair, and Mountain,* I had never worked this way. I went ahead and chose a concerto by John Field that I knew inside out before rehearsals ever started.

I had had very little formal musical training, and when I began making work in the so-called postmodern, post-Cunningham/Cage world, I thought very little about music. In the composition class with Robert and Judy Dunn in the early 1960s, we each were to make something to Satie's *Gymnopédie*. Robert Dunn was explaining the musical form.

The Mysteries & What's So Funny by David Gordon (photo Andrew Eccles)

Chair by David Gordon (photo Lois Greenfield)

I asked in my smart-ass way, "So you mean you can make the piece based on the music?"

"Yes."

"And you can make it off the music?"

"Yes."

"So, does that mean you can make it without the music and then do it with the music?"

"Yes."

"Okay, thank you."

I went away and made this piece without music and put it with music and that's the way I basically did it for the first number of years I was working. It seemed to me that if I used the music as atmosphere as opposed to as a map, I could allow myself to do whatever I wanted. So I never finished playing a piece of music. I put music in to say in some way, "Think about seeing this and hearing this," and then I took the music away. By the time I was living in the loft, I was still doing that with pieces like *Not Necessarily Recognizable Objectives*, in which, for a mightily slow floor-bound woman's trio, I use the opening waking-up music from *Fille Mal Gardée* (a Frederick Ashton ballet I'm very fond of) as a musical reference.

I began to be interested in trying to do something more or other with music about twenty years ago when I made *Trying Times* to the entire Stravinsky score for the ballet *Apollo*. I was friends with the dance critic Arlene Croce and was spending a lot of time going to the New York City Ballet with her. I saw *Apollo* a number of times, and wondered more and more how you made movement that would stand up to the power of that Stravinsky music. I decided to try. I picked the sections of the music that were the hardest for me to understand how to deal with and began working on those sections first—because if I wasn't going to be able to do those parts, the whole project would be impossible. I needed to be the most frightened to start with. I was really trying to play musical catch-up. How do you not do dumb things to music? I listened hard. I asked a lot of questions.

During this music investigation I did a concert at the Joyce Theater in which two of the pieces were *My Folks* and *A Plain Romance Explained*. Each piece had a three-minute section with the same movement rephrased for Klezmer music and a John Field nocturne. I waited to see if anyone would say anything. Nobody did.

When I got the job to make the first ABT ballet, knowing Stravinsky's admiration for Mozart, I bought a batch of Mozart recordings. I listened and listened and realized, "This guy doesn't need me to make anything. He does it all. The only thing I can do is chase him. How can I not be slavish to the music but understand and respect it? What is its character? What do

I need to do in relation to it? Do I have the need to do something perverse with it?" I'm forever asking Valda and the dancers and my stage manager Ed, who is very good about music, to explain to me what I'm hearing. "Okay, now I think what I'm hearing here is this. Is this possible? Okay, this phrase ends right here. Are you not hearing this place where the music alters slightly? I don't know what it's called. Is there another instrument? Something changes right there. Do you not hear that?" I'm a little defensive. I wish I were a little more sophisticated. I'm figuring out ways to make the music work for me.

In a recent piece, *Private Lives of Dancers*, the music for the last twenty minutes of the dance is the first section of an already existing piece called *Weather* by Michael Gordon. I determined that the best way to work on the piece was to make the movement for that twenty-minute section first—although it would be the last part of the dance. This way, rather than make a whole lot of sections and then have to find out how they would all work together, once I had the end section, I developed a series of short dances that suggested the inevitable movement material that was, in fact, already in the completed finale. I used sections of the recorded music, reduced for piano and played live, for the short dances and I added live piano to the recorded finale. It was an exhilarating process.

There was a point, in some piece of work, twenty-something years ago (maybe it was *Profile* at Dance Theater Workshop) in which I started with only four lines of spoken text. I told them to the dancers. "You say this. You say this. You say this. Just say it." Someone would say the wrong thing and then they'd say, "Oh, I'm sorry; I was supposed to say this." Then I'd say, "Okay, now you say all of that." Then they'd repeat saying first the wrong thing, then, "Oh, I'm sorry; I was supposed to say this," followed by what they were supposed to say. And I would begin to accumulate what happened in their attempts to learn the text. And if they got it right, I would give two new lines. Now they'd have to remember everything they were asked to say, everything they said that they weren't asked to say, and everything they were now being asked to say, which would force more error. The final script would be the result of what they were in fact doing in the process of trying to do it.

Eventually I could sit down and write the kind of dialogue and response which sounds like an ad lib response to an actual line, and the questioning of the ad lib, or the questioning of the line. I'd hand that all out, and then sometimes in the rehearsal process something still would happen which disrupted or disorganized the material for a moment; and if it seemed good to me, we would keep it.

I attempt to organize performance material to reference and resemble life, or at least the life I lead. I live and work in the same place on two sides of a great sliding door. On the side of the door where I live, Valda and I finish off our conversation as we enter the studio where the dancers are all having conversations about what they did last night and the train ride and breakfast and what hurts, and now I say, "Okay, let's start." At that point everything else gets put away and we do something called dancing. Over and over we walk in and interrupt a conversation and start dancing. Then one day I say, "That conversation was interesting. What if you kept that conversation going?" I ask people, "Do you think you can keep that conversation going while we begin to do this?" They are suddenly self-conscious about what they say. So I go and write the conversation. Then nobody's self-conscious.

I think my work was always personal and autobiographical, from the very beginning. I was sad and uncomfortable about not being an abstract artist, but, when Alyce Dissette became my manager about sixteen years ago she looked at the first concert I did under her management and said, "You belong in the theater." She called every theater in America and got the first workshop of *The Mysteries* (which I wrote, choreographed, and directed) at the Guthrie Theater in Minneapolis. I had my dancers, their actors, and a great rehearsal space. I had seen a version of a mock door they used that opened and closed and I asked, "Could I have a door like that? Except, could it be a swinging door and could the frame be on wheels so I can roll it any place in the space for people to go through?" They built the most wonderful dancing door. Immediately when it arrived the dancers all began dancing with the door. They rode it. They jumped through it. They tried how fast and how slow it could move. The actors all stood and watched them, and after a while I said, "Would you like to try going through the door?" They went back and forth through the door a number of times, and one woman said, "The only question I have is, when I go through this door am I entering somewhere or exiting somewhere?"

I have begun to acknowledge, since working in the theater, that essentially I am a storyteller. I've always been a storyteller. I just never told anybody what the story was. In the first Judson concert I did a piece called *Helen's Dance* (to the Satie *Gymnopédie*) in which I planted flowers and imitated the pop singer Billy Daniels doing "That Old Black Magic" without anybody being able to hear the words. The piece was named for my high school friend who died of cancer. "No, no," I claimed, "it's an abstract piece of work."

I had never told the dancers I worked with what was behind what I was asking for and I was disconcerted when I first met actors because they really asked questions. It was a new country for which I had to find a language. Back in our own studio, I sometimes talked in terms of image or the consequence of an action. I acknowledged dramatic underpinnings to the movements and the interconnected layering of the music, language, and movement. I'm not interested in "You must feel this" but I am interested in the range of feelings one might have about a set of circumstances.

While making *Private Lives of Dancers*, we spent time going through the lines. I'd say, "Okay, why do you think you're saying that to her? Do you have an agenda? Do you want her to stop dancing? Do you want that part for yourself? Would that make a difference in how you say this line?" I don't assume this process makes the work more accessible but it enriches the life that's going on in the dance and in the words themselves. Somebody is actually thinking, rather than just memorizing some words in relation to two steps and a turn. Two things are going on simultaneously instead of two things being glued together. It's important to me.

The Mysteries & What's So Funny, first produced in May 1991 at the Spoleto Festival in South Carolina, tracks the histories of Marcel Duchamp and Dada and my dada, and mama too. I'd been working on the script for about a year. I called my parents, Rose and Sam, and said, "I'm coming to read to you." When I got there, my father, who was not well, lay on the couch and my mother, who was not well, sat on a chair. I said, "Your names are in here. There's family history. If you're uncomfortable, I'll use other names." I opened the script and proceeded to read the entire bloody thing, and they both fell fast asleep as soon as I started. At the very end I closed the book noisily. My mother woke up and said, "That's wonderful. Are you hungry?" My father woke up and said, "Who would want to see a thing like that?"

I never said publicly that the play was autobiographical, and my son Ain noticed that the word "Jew" was never used. "Well," I said, "I thought the play was about a class of people, not a religion."

"Oh, sure," he said.

Then, in 1994 he and I wrote a play together called *The Family Business* about a series of drastic family events that he'd been unhappily in the center of, and he said, "We have to use the word 'Jew.'"

"I worry that labels are limiting," I said.

"You don't worry about 'old' or 'blonde.'"

"Some labels are more limiting than others," I said.

"'Jew' is important to the story. It's a cultural reference."

So I gave in. I've been fighting labels since the Judson. No, I wasn't a Judson artist; I did not share a group aesthetic. I was an artist at the Judson. No, I wasn't postmodern; Yvonne invented that for herself. No, I am not a comic artist. No, I am not an improvisational artist. No, I'm not a Jewish artist. I am an artist reinventing himself every time out of the gate if he's lucky. I am an artist (born Jewish) who uses everything that ever happened to me and everything that ever happened to you if you let me.

I think invention is great. But there's desperation in too much invention. I don't like to eat in restaurants in which you're going to get a piece of fish with cinnamon raison squash puree topped with radish relish. Take your hands off that fish. Leave it alone! I'm not interested in actors for whom transformation means they have to invent a limp, a nose, half an accent, and a recurring gesture. Too many things! If I can make a difference with less going on, what would that be? Take one person out of that symmetrical group? If something has value, if it matters, then you give it its due. You respect it. You get a sense of what it means. You establish a relationship. You don't misuse it or attempt to disguise it as something else. You have respect for the simplest relation to a piece of material. That doesn't mean you can't turn it upside down. You can turn it upside down because you are looking to see if the underbelly is equally interesting and evocative.

I use some objects over and over—the rolling door, the frame, the chair—and continue to be surprised at what they can do. I never liked ladders. Ladders always seem corny onstage. Umbrellas, too. But I used ladders in *Firebugs*. I turned the Greek chorus into a gang of firemen who scrambled and tumbled out of a mini–fire truck in a sawdust-covered ring like a circus act. The ladders we used were the kind meant to lean up against a wall. But there was no wall, so the actors and dancers had to support each other and balance the ladder as best they could as they climbed. They went up as far as they could go before the ladder started to fall. A lovely metaphor.

New York City
March 7, 2003

4
Trisha Brown (b. 1936)

Trisha Brown was born in Aberdeen, Washington, where in her youth she studied tap, ballet, acrobatics, and jazz. At Mills College she took courses in dance composition based on Louis Horst's approach and studied with Horst himself at the American Dance Festival at Connecticut College. It was there that she witnessed John Cage's lecture on indeterminacy, which she says tipped the scales toward her engagement in choreography. After getting her degree in modern dance from Mills, Brown studied task-based improvisation, vocalization, and experiential anatomy at Anna Halprin's studio. At the urging of Simone Forti and Yvonne Rainer, Brown moved to New York City, where she continued to study modern dance and took Robert Dunn's composition class based on the teachings of John Cage.

"Each one of these encounters etched its message somewhere inside of me as I passed through," Brown says. "I am a rigorous choreographer. I think that comes from Mills and Horst. I have a sense of esprit and a playful irreverent streak. I think that comes from Halprin. And from John Cage it was just the sheer glory of making art. He was the first one that made that clear to me."

Trisha Brown's earliest works were presented in the Judson Dance Theater and utilized improvisational solutions to scores. She went on to make dances for unused spaces: walking on walls, down the sides of buildings, and relaying movements across New York City rooftops. Balancing a strong structural imagination and a fanciful delight in movement, Brown has undertaken a new focus for her work every few years. Working in cycles has allowed her to delve into structural issues rooted in the way the dancers relate to each other, to the space, and to music. Her loose-limbed, sequential movements play elusively against her formal explorations.

She formed the Trisha Brown Company in 1970 and continues to show her work internationally. In recent years Brown has focused more on working with music and has had commissions to choreograph operas.

Among her honors, the French government named her *Chevalier dans l'Ordre des Arts et des Lettres* and she has received a MacArthur "Genius" Award, five fellowships from the National Endowment for the Arts, two John Simon Guggenheim Fellowships, the New York State Governor's Arts Award, two New York Dance and Performance (Bessie) Awards, the National Medal of Art, and numerous honorary doctorates.

* * *

Trisha Brown (photo Lois Greenfield)

Trisha Brown

Speaking in all humility, I have an amazing body. It was a gift. I didn't make it go this way. It doesn't even really belong to me, although I'm in charge of it. My cousins and sisters and brothers all have it. So do my mom and dad. They're all in sports. The sequential movement that comes out of my body I can see in a nephew playing ping pong, the way he pulls his wrist back. There's a lot of what we used to call "English" on the movement. A physical instrument such as my body wants to move. It has to move. It moves. Had sports been more available, I probably would have gone in that direction. I just had this piece of machinery that was looking for a driver, a pilot.

There are myths that I levitated in the early years, when I was at Mills College. When no one was looking I did something close to it. I would burst into the air and go up and try to get two or three other places before I came down, leading out with my head and counteracting with a leg thrusting up and reaching down to the floor. I always landed like a cat, but the trajectory of the movement was like little explosions.

During the Judson era from 1960 to 1967, I was working in a collective of brilliant people. If you have my kind of a body and you are working with other people who are giving you extremely sensitive and stimulating things to do, amazing things to do, daring things to do, you're on the edge of your capability and you're not sure you even should be out there doing any of it. But on the other hand it's totally thrilling. My colleagues were breathtaking: Steve Paxton and Bob Rauschenberg of course, the Grand Union experience, and David Gordon improvising. There was an irreverence in that period, but also a sense of competition and challenge. So many, many gauntlets were thrown down, with people racing to pick them up. It was an audacious, anarchic time of "whatever you give me, I'll twist it, baby."

And yet they weren't asking me to do what I knew I could do. I found myself remembering what I know physically, and yearning for it, wanting to do it. I never thought I would be a choreographer; I always thought I was going to be a dancer because I didn't have mentoring in the direction of choreography. I wonder if I had known where I would be now whether I would have taken it on.

In making dances I work in cycles. I pursue a cycle over a period of two or three years. This is my habit from Judson on, until the present. You can go back and look at the "Equipment Pieces" in the early seventies where I walked down the sides of buildings. Then there was the "Mathematic" series: accumulation of gestures, deaccumulation, reaccumulation. After that, *Locus* in 1975 was a grid with an aleatoric score that told me where to move in space right around my body, not traveling, just stationary. That was followed by a period of exploration, trying to find what my vocabulary is vis-à-vis everyone else in the world.

Coming out of that, the next cycle was working with an improvisational system of capturing and repeating what I had improvised with a group of people. That process gave the 1983 *Set and Reset* an "Unstable Molecular Structure," meaning that each one of us as a dancer was on the same phrase, but we were acting like independent molecules and were overlaying each other with the same material. I saw it as a layered phrase of shared impulses. There's an uncanniness to the look of it and people want to know, "Is this improvised?" Well, originally it was, but then we memorized it. I found a way to do that. You improvise in small increments. And you go back and repeat it and repeat it until you get it. Then you can go on improvisationally. You don't do a long improvisation. I could never recall all of that. And even in the small increments you lose some of the nuanced, elusive aspect of it—like what caused you to do what you did and therefore gave you the timing and the quality of it.

In the "Valiant" series of the mid-eighties I ran an intervention on my natural way of moving by making hard, harsh, sharp-lined, angular, geometric movement, and compositionally working with small units like duets and trios, and then interfacing those units. That was a three-year cycle. Because of the harsh, powerful movement, it was just too much for my company to do all the pieces in that cycle in one program. They were backstage barfing. So they begged me, "Trisha, please…." "Back to Zero," then, in response to the dancers' plight, was very simple. It was an investigation of subconscious movement. I just let gestures happen without thinking about them at all. I thought it would be terribly embarrassing to do in front of my dancers, but they loved it. I made a couple of "Back to Zero" pieces.

Eventually I went into music because I wanted to direct opera. So I imposed that cycle. I just said to myself, "What haven't you done yet, girl?" And I came up with directing an opera. I had had experience with opera in 1986 as a choreographer for Lina Wertmuller's direction of *Carmen*. But in that situation, I wasn't in control; I could only run my interventions when she allowed me to. But I loved opera. So I got back to it in 1998, coming up through Bach and Webern to Monteverdi. And since then I have done a contemporary opera by the composer Salvatore Sciarrino. Now I'm doing a choreographed quartet to his music that's going to be premiered in Montpellier in June [2002].

There was a period as a young choreographer when I thought that dance alone was enough. My analogy was when you look at a piece of sculpture or a painting you don't need to hear music, do you? Of course, if you're walking down the side of a building, you're not putting music with it. But you are hearing something, other things. I was deeply involved in the sound of nothing or in the sound of my dancers approaching me from upstage when I'm downstage. I treasured the communication, the signaling that goes on between dancers in a tightly organized ensemble when you have no music to tell you where you are. I treasured the silence and the sound of our being present and dancing. It went so much against the convention of how one views dance; but dance viewed with music and viewed on its own are two separate things. And I became very sensitive to the perception of choreography with and without music. So even then I was working with the relationship of music and dancing—though I wasn't letting you hear the music. I was still seeing it in my dancing. It was complex, subtle, deep, a very rich experience for me.

Yet when I went back into music I was astonished how much I knew and understood about it. For my first Bach piece—which was a piece of work for this girl to do—I taught myself early polyphonic composition. I had to. I was always working with structure in my own work, so I set out to learn what the composer's structure was. When I'm working with music, I do the research on the music first and, in the case of opera and *lieder*, on the text. I'm working with these languages: music, poetry, and the body, all three engaged in telling a story. Or not.

I also was "outed" as a visual artist when my opera, Monteverdi's *Orfeo,* was appearing in Aix-en-Provence in France in 1998. I had an exhibition of my drawings in Marseille, and in a theater nearby my company was performing the same weekend. Since then my life has been impossible. I have drawn a little since then, but there is no way I can work in all those areas at the same time. I just can't get to everything. So, recently, I took on the task of an intimate piece for a museum or gallery setting for which I am working with music, dance, and drawing. I will perform three solos in it. I can do one and a half of them at this point and I have to perform them all in four weeks. Huge sheets of paper will be on the floor. I'll carry my dancing down into the paper, draw in charcoal and pastel while I'm down, and rise up and do a set form and an improvised form. Then I'll hit the paper again. Something like that. I don't know what it will be. The whole piece will be forty-five minutes long. I conceive of it as "watching Trisha think."

When I start a new piece, I run down certain issues of composition which bring with them the necessity of a new vocabulary to service the composition. First I make a handful of phrases, each of which has a different character because I want to put them in counterpoint with each other when it comes to the period of mixing. For the last quartet that I made I improvised phrases; for *El Trilogy* in 2000 I also improvised the material. So my body is still actively on a roll. And then I start to select out with my assistant, Carolyn Lucas. We select out that which is most significant to me and to the world, that is, what I assume outside people will also want to see. All the time the dancers are learning those phrases, I'm studying the movements and saying, "What am I going to do with this?" And I get a list of ideas for how I could turn this stuff on its ear once it's been presented as thematic material.

For the most recent quartet, *Geometry of Quiet*, I made the phrases last April [2001] when I got back from making the opera *Luci Mie Traditrici*, by composer Salvatore Sciarrino. I wanted duets. Other combinations and relationships accumulated out of that. I wanted the dancers each to start on a different phrase or a different place in a phrase and to intimately interlock the movement in some way with the person that they were working with. But if they hit into material that had its own impulse, material that was interesting, they were to go off on a tangent, to branch out of the thematic phrase into something else and see what we get. I have to give them license to use their creative impulses. As it turned out, I was the one in the beginning who stopped them and said, "Do this, do that." In one moment with the male dancer standing behind the female dancer, I talked them through the next action. "Put her foot up against your chest. Keep contact with that foot; drop down to the floor; go underneath her with the foot still there and let her leg mechanically rise through." So here's her leg; his body, his chest is attached to that; as his body is dropping down, is sitting down, is on the floor, is skootching forward, is rising up, her leg comes up and, from beneath, he comes through. It's just beautiful. It was very emotional. A long phrase for the duet ensued out of that intervention. Two moments of the phrase came together. Everyone in the room went, "Oh my God." And I realized I couldn't do less after that, which really slowed me down. I needed to get that timbre of feeling—through abstraction—which is always present, triggering responses in the viewer for which you don't see the cause though you are feeling the effect. It's a tender piece all the way through. It's dear. I want to say, "The soft collision of two different phrases guided off the track." Something like that. I love words too, it's true. So that's the most recent way I made a piece. I have made pieces every way I could think of, the whole gamut.

It's sometimes hard to finish a piece in the time we have. I had only eleven weeks to make *Rapture* in *El Trilogy* and I had nine weeks to make *Groove*, the third part. That's not enough time to make two full pieces. The first two weeks of the nine-week period were spent correcting the eleven-week period. So I had seven weeks to make *Groove*, and when *Groove* was finished I did make some corrections. I was literally standing on a chair in the gymnasium at Skidmore College belting out, "Phrase C, downstage right, downstage left; phrase B, left stage, left stage." I was just barking at them, mounting an attack on the stage. It was a big gas. It got videotaped, so it could be reiterated, straightened out, freshened up. Later on I also did some revisal of the improvisation in *Rapture* when I saw that I could give the dancers more structure than I had.

I know how to make a Trisha Brown choreography very well. Built into that are ways that I have assuaged my fear and feelings of insecurity over time. The younger Trisha Brown was scared to death to approach the creation of material that would spew out options for what to do next because I knew that I had to kill all of them but one. Now I know I just have to move on. There are always a lot of options. I try this one; I try that one; and each one makes more. The first one was good enough by anyone else's standards. So I've taught myself not to be lured into invention and to be more strict. But it means cutting down the deep pleasure of creation at any given moment.

So that's the accumulation of material, which is fraught with invention and is a process I adore; then there's putting that material into counterpoint with other phrases. You can go on trying this phrase with that one, that one with this one. I think the first statement I said of killing off the choices gives you an idea of what I go through emotionally.

Do my movement and my thinking have an intimate connection? First of all, I don't think my body doesn't think. My body has a strong voice and it does things that I observe. Working in improvisation with the musician Dave Douglas on *El Trilogy*, I improvised my whole heart out to a percussion score because he had commissions coming in so fast he couldn't get the new music to me. I had to go ahead. But I didn't want to be linked to a melody because then the movement wouldn't look good with the music I did get in the end. The percussion grid gave me a lot of impetus and was neutral. I actually did sixty-six goes on that percussion score. Out of that we picked thirty. They were not all long; some were really short.

That was back when I sort of got to know who I am *now* as a dancer—because I have not been the same body and mind throughout all the decades of my life. The one I found there seemed driven by a fifteen-year-old who was in the control tower, passing information on, "You've already done it to that side twice, move it. Move it somewhere else." It's so charming that my body and my mind could work together that well. One, the mind, was composing; the other was composing also, but from a physical freedom that the mind was not going to allow—at least not as soon as it caught up with what was going on, which might be after the fact. But it was really an interesting experience. It's like trying to get the control tower out at the airport to land itself.

I fully understand it's totally important to have a body of work, but I don't go back and fool around with earlier work. I don't have time; I don't have any interest. Although I love my repertory, it irritates me because it takes time to maintain. It's in competition with the creation of new work. Everyone wants the new work in its first few years of serious touring; then it sits on somebody's list somewhere. We are, however, reconstructing old operas. We just reconstructed the *Orfeo* in Brussels in April [2002]. It premiered in May. We had a reconstruction of the second opera, *Luci Mie Traditrici*. That's a big work. It's not in the dance company; it's performed by singers. There are only a few of us that work at maintaining the operas, and I'm one of them. My assistant is one of them. Different people, first from inside of the company but now from outside of the company, form little teams that go out and try to reteach the movement material to the singers because the singers are constantly replaced. It's a tremendous affirmation of the success of this work that it's constantly in reconstruction, but it's awfully difficult for us to service it.

All the dancers who have come into my company have gone through a crisis of reorganizing how their bodies work. There are a lot of people around to support them in that crisis because they've all been through it. I look for the ultimate machine, a person who can work in a multilayered gesturing process. The dancers have to be precise. They need to give the amount of musculation to the gesture that sees it through to the end without any more or any less than is wanted. They need a kind of groundedness and centeredness.

I've a lot of feelings about the reciprocity of creation in the making of a dance. I don't ask my dancers to go make the phrases for me; but what they're capable of doing, what their excellences are, disparate and arising unpredictably from moment to moment, that's what the audience is going to see. Because I'm making it on them and for them, their very beings are in trade. And that's reciprocity. That's how deeply they are in it. For many years I knew a piece was finished when I cried seeing it, because I knew that we had done a lot of work together, but that this phase of working was over. My dancers were heroic and I loved them for that.

Set and Reset by Trisha Brown (photo Chris Callis)

Five Part Weather Invention by Trisha Brown (photo Chris Callis)

I've become deeply involved in collaboration in the last fifteen years. The first principle in collaboration is that you have an ally in what you're going to do. The discussion begins with the invitation to the designer. I almost always, with a few exceptions, select an artist that I know and whose work I admire, of course, and with whom I feel comfortable as a friend. I started in the beginning of my career to alternate from year to year having a man and a woman as composer or designer. I always try to do that, even if no one else notices.

I chose Bob Rauschenberg to do the first set for me, for *Glacial Decoy* in 1979. He's a big intrusion on life itself. He's a huge personality. On the other hand, he has enormous sensory equipment, and I found that we were thinking alike without any previous conversation about the subject. Thinking of the influence on me from Cage, Cunningham, and—through them—from Rauschenberg, there was already a kinship. I had been showing my pieces in galleries and museums. I invited Bob to join me when I "passed through the proscenium arch onto the great stage of illusion." Bob knew about costume and sets; he was accomplished in these areas and yet a kindred spirit in art making. Even so, we often collided. It happens. I thought I was right. He thought he was right. We duked it out and got all of our issues out and picked the best solution, jointly.

For instance, I did not want to be nude under my costume. I thought a little pair of panties might be nice. Had I known I was not going to have underwear beneath a translucent costume, I wouldn't have kicked my leg so high facing the audience. Simple things like that. But they are aesthetic issues. He liked the sensuality of the body dancing that he could see up close in the intimate studio space. He wanted to reproduce it in a 2,000-seat house. That was his issue. It is like "stripping the bride bare," revealing the body, giving the body to the audience. I argued for lighting that would give us the sense of concealment that I needed, and revealment, which I also needed since one of my subjects in *Set and Reset* was privacy and non-privacy, conceal and reveal.

The trust between the designer, the composer, and the choreographer is a complex subject. I do the best choreography I can and I want the look and sound to support its being the most significant work I can make at this stage of my career. I can be convinced. I know a better idea when I hear one. But I can also be totally recalcitrant if I'm losing the thing I consider precious. I think the deepest connection between Bob and me is the shared sensibility, which includes recklessness and structure. I'm structured; he's reckless! But I'm reckless, too, if I can shape it, if it has a logic, and I have an argument for including it. I don't like gratuitous recklessness or irreverence. Or up to a point I do.

Aesthetic showdowns occurred throughout the period—sometimes quietly and sometimes of volcanic proportions. But there were simple things I could do to dodge around someone else's incursion on my aesthetic. I could mediate what they did by what I could do on top of it. So it catalyzes creativity. It's a shared process, a give-and-take in which all of us try to get the best level of production we can.

I'm working on Schubert's *Winterreise* for a singer and three of my dancers. We did a workshop before I went to Brussels in April. Now we're coming back to it. I started working on Tuesday again. A lot of the material has been created. Now it has to get learned and separated and associated with this music, or not, or be cast out. All of the processes of selection have to happen. But what I basically did on Tuesday was to jump off a cliff not knowing. That's central. I'm currently at the step where I am mixing what we call the movement cells—the units of subject relevant to the poetry—and sorting out which cell goes with which song. A cell is like a small, thematic consolidation of information that represents the narrative and has to be brought into close approximation with the music that best presents the narrative, albeit in an abstract language. And anything can happen here. Basically what I'm doing is jumping off a cliff. And sometime next December the critics will tell us whether I landed on my feet or not.

New York City
May 31, 2002

5
Lucinda Childs (b. 1940)

Lucinda Childs grew up in New York City, where she took classes in both dance and acting. Her experience studying with Helen Tamiris at the Perry-Mansfield summer school and a later master class with Merce Cunningham turned her finally toward dance. Childs majored in dance at Sarah Lawrence College, where she studied with the renowned composition teacher Bessie Schönberg and with Cunningham dancer Judith Dunn. She knew even then that the work of Merce Cunningham and the Judson Dance Theater particularly interested her. Immediately after graduating in 1962 she became active with the Judson group as a choreographer and performer. Her work with them was mostly solos based on an uninflected, gestural use of ordinary objects, sometimes including spoken monologues. She took a five-year break from dance starting in 1968.

In 1973 Childs resumed choreographing and established the Lucinda Childs Dance Company. The use of geometrical floor patterns as the structuring premise of her work dates from that time, with dancers moving along straight lines and arcs of circles. Her dances are recognizable by upright bodies performing subtle variations of insistently rhythmic traveling phrases that often include steps, skips, leaps, and turns. The clarity and precision of her work has remained even as her work has taken on other theatrical components. Partly as a result of her 1976 collaboration with Robert Wilson, the designer of stark and strikingly imagistic avant-garde theatrical works, and the minimalist composer Philip Glass, Childs in 1978 began choreographing to music. For years her preference was for composers such as Glass and John Adams, whose repetitive variations mirrored her own choreographic method. Collaborations with visual artists such as Sol Lewitt and Frank Gehry followed.

In recent years Childs has given up her own company and has focused on choreographing for ballet and opera companies in the United States and in Europe, where she has had commissions from the Lyon Opera Ballet, Paris Opera Ballet, and Rambert Dance Company and has had her work performed by the Bavarian State Opera Ballet in Munich, Maggio Danza in Florence, Les Ballets de Monte-Carlo in Monaco, and the Ballet de l'Opéra de Genève, among others. She is the recipient of an Obie Award and a John Simon Guggenheim Fellowship and was honored in 1997 with the appointment to the rank of *Officier des Arts et des Lettres* in France.

* * *

Lucinda Childs (photo Kishin Shinoyama)

Lucinda Childs

Growing up in New York City, I first attended the King-Coit School to study acting and dancing. I have a vivid memory from age eleven when the famous ballerina Tanaquil LeClercq from the New York City Ballet was one of our guest teachers. It was like a dream to be her student and naturally I wanted to try to do everything perfectly, but found it not possible. Later on, when the actress Mildred Dunnock came to visit the school and encouraged me, I decided that I wanted to be an actress. During summer vacations, I went to the Perry-Mansfield school of theatre and dance in Colorado and took dance class with Harriet Ann Gray and Helen Tamiris. I also studied with theater director Barney Brown from the Pasadena Playhouse in California. When I returned for my second year, I auditioned for Tamiris, who chose me to be in a trio with Daniel Nagrin. The following summer, in 1959, I went to Colorado College to study dance and composition with Hanya Holm.

When I got to Sarah Lawrence College, I wanted to continue to study both acting and dancing, but after Merce Cunningham came to teach a master class I changed my mind and began to focus exclusively on dance training. During my college years, I took classes at the Cunningham Studio in New York and, at the suggestion of one of my teachers, went to see performances of Yvonne Rainer. Yvonne was a founding member of the Judson Dance Theater—which I joined after graduating from college in 1962. As a dance major at Sarah Lawrence, I was able to study both technique and composition. In that way, before moving back to New York, I had the experience of working on my own compositions and the chance to explore and develop my own ideas. While I was studying at the Cunningham Studio, Yvonne Rainer encouraged me to show my work at the weekly Judson workshops. The solo I showed there, *Pastime,* was then performed at the Judson Memorial Church in 1963.

During the next few years I worked for the most part as a soloist, but also performed in works by other choreographers from the Judson group, as well as in the dance companies of Joyce Trisler, James Waring, Merle Marsicano, Aileen Passloff, and Beverly Schmidt. At the end of the Judson period, around 1966, following the famous *Nine Evenings: Experiments in Art and Technology*—a presentation of collaborations between choreographers and technicians from Bell Laboratories—I wanted to take my work in a new direction. I did not particularly want to go on as a soloist making the kind of dances that I had made at Judson, so I took some time to work on my own and to explore what was going on in New York in the realm of painting and sculpture. This was an enormously stimulating time, as one could observe the emerging world of pop art together with the advent of the minimalist aesthetic. I had already been acquainted with the work of Jackson Pollock and Barnett Newman. Mark Rothko, too, was extremely important to me. These artists could not be categorized simply as abstract expressionists or minimalists. I was also deeply impressed by the works of Jasper Johns and Robert Rauschenberg, who designed décor and costumes for Merce Cunningham's choreography.

The vision of these artists doubtless influenced my work. When I started my company in 1973, I was interested in creating dances with simple, geometrical spatial patterns. My 1976 *Radial Courses* is a quartet designed on the floor plan of four overlapping circles. I was interested in exploring what would happen when two dancers paced an eighteen-count phrase on a semicircular path while the other two dancers were executing a phrase of the same duration on a floor pattern that covered three quarters of a circle. I wondered where they would meet up if they went in opposite directions. The best way to figure this out was to make notations in the form of a diagrammatical score in which I drew each dancer's path with a different color. Even though there were only two phrases and two spatial patterns, I found that there was an infinite number of ways to work within these limitations. The only sound for these dances was the dancers' footsteps. The musical sensibility was sustained by the consistent tempo that the dancers had to maintain among themselves—a rigorous task in and of itself.

During the seventies and some of the eighties, everything I choreographed was notated with diagrammatic scores that I designed for each dance and that enabled me to reconstruct any of my dances at any time. After setting myself strict limitations, I would often discover unexpected surprises. My 1976 solo *Mix Detail* was one of the biggest revelations. It was constructed as an accumulation on a simple grid pattern; but I wasn't able to understand why the dance never ended where it started until, by drawing it out, I found that the distance of one pace was gained consistently more in one direction than in any of the others.

It was the tradition of the Ballets Russes in the early twentieth century to have contemporary artists, contemporary musicians, and contemporary painters collaborate with the choreographers of that time. This was one of the most exciting periods in dance. In our time, I found that this same tradition of collaboration was also happening with Cunningham and his collaborators John Cage, Jasper Johns, Andy Warhol, Roy Lichtenstein, Robert Rauschenberg, and others. I took a step in this direction myself after collaborating with Robert Wilson and Philip Glass on their opera *Einstein on the Beach*.

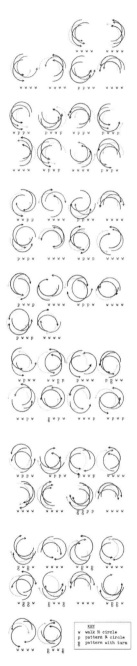

Chart of **Radial Courses** by Lucinda Childs

Up to that time I had only presented my work in so-called alternative spaces: churches, museums, galleries, sidewalks. But from the first time I saw Robert Wilson's *A Letter to Queen Victoria* in New York in 1974, I wanted to work with him. I was fascinated with the way he transformed and extended the stage space with lighting and the way his extraordinary architectural designs redefined the proscenium space. Our collaboration also permitted me to revisit the realm of acting, since as a performer in his opera I had a speaking role. *Einstein on the Beach* premiered in France at the Festival d'Avignon in 1976 and had its first New York performance at the Metropolitan Opera House.

Einstein marked another important transition for me: For the first time I was working with a composer. I studied his score. Then—for my solo in Act One, *Character on Three Diagonals*—I choreographed a series of accumulative phrases in such a way that the accents in the movement didn't always coincide with the downbeat of the musical phrase. During *Einstein*, Philip Glass suggested that we continue to work together, so we created *Dance* in 1979. Since I choreographed *Dance* after Philip's music had been composed, I first analyzed how his music was constructed and I designed my own structure to interact with it. I found that the structures that we use are very similar, and it was interesting and challenging to consider how to put them together. The counterpoint in Philip's scores can be analyzed numerically into groups of two- and three-count phrases. At first my dancers found it very hard to memorize, although they liked the challenge and the concentration of working with Philip's music. "Oh, is that a five or is that a six?" they would ask. They could easily get lost because my structure was not always exactly reflecting his. The two structures were designed to come together at certain points, however, so there were sections and landmarks to go back to. I have continued to work with Philip's music and the music of John Adams in this way.

To complete the collaboration for *Dance*, we turned to visual artist Sol LeWitt, who created a film décor for the piece. In watching rehearsals, LeWitt chose certain parts of the dance to film in 35 millimeter black and white. Some sequences were filmed as long shots, some as close-ups, and some from overhead. The film was projected onto a screen that filled the entire downstage proscenium space in front of the dancers, who were visible behind it. In editing the film, LeWitt used a number of different techniques to combine the dancers on stage with those in the film, the most frequent being a horizontal split-level. In this way the dancers on stage were seen directly below the same dancers in the film. For my solo section, the projection screen was split vertically and shot from opposite angles, so I'm seen on film from the front and back simultaneously. This

work continues to be performed and has just recently entered the repertory of the Ballet de l'Opéra du Rhin in France.

In the seventies and eighties, geometric patterns completely dominated
the structure of the dances I made. But now I'm freer to work with patterns spontaneously, that is, without meticulous preparation, because I've
worked in this way for so many years. Also my work has expanded as I've
adapted to new dimensions in collaborating with visual artists. For example, the architect Frank Gehry designed a split-level stage for my dance
Available Light. Having one level above the other gave the thrill of watching a dancer above picking up on another's movement below. John Adams
was the composer for this project and it was his first musical composition
for dance. Since then he has composed music for the New York City Ballet.
I also choreographed Adams's *Chamber Symphony* in 1993 even though it
was not written as a ballet.

After many years of creating works with the music of John Adams and
Philip Glass and with composers in that idiom—such as Jon Gibson, Robert Galasso, and Michael Nyman—I wanted to explore outside the minimalist aesthetic and gravitated toward the music of György Ligeti. He
seemed an obvious choice for my type of choreography because of the
kind of classicism that's fundamental to his music and because of the way
his music is constructed, so full of wonderful rhythms and syncopations. I
found that a continuum of movement could be built into the rhythmic
patterns that he had created.

I met with Ligeti in Paris in 1984 and asked him if he would consider
composing for dance. Later that year, when he visited my studio in New
York, he suggested that I meet with the harpsichord player, Elizabeth
Chojnacka, for whom he had dedicated a number of works including
Hungarian Rock, which I used in the opening to my 1991 *Rhythm Plus.* Ms.
Chonjacka also introduced me to the music of many other contemporary
European composers, such as Iannis Xenakis and Henryk Górecki, and
played their works with my company on tour for a period of nine years
between 1991 and 2000.

Even when I'm working with music that isn't specifically minimalist,
I find that there's always a structure and a sequencing in the musical
score that I can follow. I studied piano as student, so I can analyze a
musical score very quickly and condense it into my own kind of nota-
tion. That way I can have all the information I need on one single page
and can refer to it in rehearsal without ever having to look at the musical score. Even so, I like to first listen to the chosen music in an open-
ended fashion without attempting to formulate a structure and without

even keeping track of what goes through my head. It's a very pleasurable period. Then I find that the form I develop for the choreography takes shape more or less intuitively after I have become familiar with the music. What I choose to do depends on what kind of structure the music has, how many sections there are in the music, and whether or not I want to follow the musical structure or make another one.

When I'm making a new work, the rehearsals generally are four hours long and continue for around six weeks. First I work alone, improvising for a period of time. This process is completely intuitive but disciplined. I mean, I could improvise forever, but the point is to capture and retain the things that I would like to develop further with the dancers in rehearsal. I set some material, then build on what I have or move on to something else. I don't abandon the material that interests me until it has crystallized into a form that I can go back to.

I find that making the movement phrases is now more than ever the most time-consuming part of the process. I like to work out all of the phrases on my own and to build variations. That way, the dancers can start out with one phrase but I can also teach them a second version that evolved out of the first. I also like to put a second variation with the first variation, combining them in different ways, creating a counterpoint. I can overlap the phrases or stagger them in various ways. I work that out with the dancers in rehearsal. I know beforehand what I want to try to do, but am ready to adjust immediately in rehearsal—to restructure and try different ways of combining phrases. Teaching the material to the dancers helps me to get a better grasp on the ways it can be used. At that point problem solving can be spontaneous. So by the time everybody in the company has danced the new material, I've already begun to select a scenario for piecing the material together. I revise as I go along and tend not to move on to new material until a section is complete.

Rehearsal is a process of discovery. Nothing really coalesces for me until I'm actually in rehearsal with the dancers. Only then can I set the right combinations of phrases. I can go into the studio with preconceived ideas and come out with nothing having worked the way I thought it would. Part of the fascination is that when something doesn't look right, a minor change, like changing a dancer's facing by a quarter turn, will make all the difference. These simple things can be easily overlooked but are so important.

One and One by Lucinda Childs (photo Peter Perazio)

Concerto by Lucinda Childs (photo Peter Perazio)

I no longer maintain my own company. These days, as a guest choreographer working with other companies, I ask for auditions to be held well in advance. I also like to do a workshop to let the dancers really get a sense of my movement style. Once the dancers are chosen, during the first week of rehearsal I tend to jump around from section to section so that they can try out the different dynamics of the movement. I select movement sequences that I feel will best illustrate what I'm striving for. This process gives me a sense of their individual movement qualities, which then helps me decide which dancers will do which material. I can't always come in and cast the specific roles the first day. It can take time, but once the casting is settled, I go back and start at the beginning of one section and construct very carefully from there.

The process is both frightening and thrilling. I never get around the anxiety I feel before I start to work; it's always there. I never know how rehearsal will go on a given day. I might come into the studio and give the dancers something which they find very hard, so I have to drop it and go on to something else, but then I go back to it the next day and try it again. By then of course I've thought about it and asked myself, "Why is that so difficult?" I analyze it and think it through so that when I try it again, it works. I find that process very exciting and reassuring. It's difficult trying something new for the first time—although sometimes the new material ends up being one of the better parts of the ballet and something that the dancers enjoy once they get it. Some of the European companies I work with are resistant to the complicated counts and so much memorization. But by now many of the companies in Europe have performed the ballets of choreographers such as William Forsythe, so they've already been exposed to a kind of work which is extremely demanding and which requires a lot of patience.

My first invitation to choreograph outside my company was in 1981, when I was invited to choreograph a new work for the Groupe de Recherche Chorégraphique de l'Opéra de Paris. This was an experimental group that had volunteered to work with experimental choreographers such as myself. I made a work titled *Mad Rush* with music by Philip Glass. The dancers picked up on my movement style quite well since the vocabulary that I use is essentially classically based. When the Pacific Northwest Ballet invited me to Seattle in 1984 to choreograph *Cascade*, I first demonstrated all of the steps in jazz shoes. Later on some of the women asked me if they could try some of the variations on pointe. We tried it and decided, yes, that the ballet would be done on pointe. It was interesting to learn more from them about what can and cannot be done on pointe and why. Some of my steps—such as the strong *fouetté* movement that makes a complete half turn without any preparation—were feasible, depending on where the dancer's weight was. But there were difficulties in their having to do so much *piqué* and *relevé* work on pointe. And some movements were just not possible. I had to work it out and therefore learned a tremendous amount. Sometimes I'd say, "Oh, this will be easy; here we go." And no, it was a disaster. At other times I'd say, "Oh, this will probably be impossible." And it was fine.

During the past ten years I've also had offers to work as a choreographer for opera. The first one was "The Dance of the Seven Veils" for Richard Strauss's *Salome* in 1992, commissioned for the Salzburg Festival in Austria. It was interesting for me because it wasn't just a ten-minute sequence where Salome suddenly does a dance that's unrelated to anything else. I worked closely with the director and we used different elements of the dance throughout the entire opera. There's a demand now to improve the visual aspect of opera, which means that the singers are required to move more. I try to develop movement for them in a collaborative way that makes sense to them and supports them as singers. Once again I'm obliged to work within strict limitations, but I find the restrictions to be an interesting stimulus.

Every new work is a new challenge for me, and deliberately so. When I chose to choreograph *Daphnis and Chlöe* to the music of Maurice Ravel, it was because, of all the dances from the Ballets Russes period, it was the least known in its original form. There are no records of the movement from the original version choreographed by Michel Fokine, only photographs and images of the Leon Bakst décor and costumes. Also, following the ten-year period of working with so many opera composers, I felt ready to approach a romantically classical score for a full-length ballet, and to discover ways to combine my contemporary aesthetic with the wonderfully complex score of Ravel. *Daphnis* premiered with the Geneva Opera ballet in spring 2002.

Finances are a big issue. At the end of the Judson period in the 1960s there was no National Endowment for the Arts to support dance. It was hard then to know how to raise money and support myself. I began to teach first grade in the New York City public school system. As much as I appreciated the financial independence, I found that it consumed too much of my time and after a few years I gave it up so that I could return to dance and focus on choreography. When I left the public schools in the early seventies, it was possible to get choreography fellowships from the National Endowment for the Arts—which made a big difference. But it still remained very difficult to pay the dancers or myself in any substantial way.

When support for dance companies increased during the eighties, my choreography began to be presented at the Brooklyn Academy of Music and eventually my company was able to self-produce a number of seasons at the Joyce Theater. But this support gradually diminished as a result of the controversy over the 1989 Corcoran Gallery exhibition of Robert Mapplethorpe's photographs. I felt compelled to address the censorship issue and wrote letters of protest against the cancellation of the exhibition to Senator Alfonse D'Amato and to John Frohnmayer, who was the head of the National Endowment for the Arts—to no avail. As the financial situation for American artists declined, I was able to keep a small company together by virtue of the invitations that we received to tour in Europe.

In the year 2000 my company celebrated its twenty-fifth anniversary season at the Brooklyn Academy of Music's Harvey Theater. We also toured in Europe, with presentations of my company at the *Festival de la Danse* in Montpellier, France, and a fifth season at the Théâtre de la Ville in Paris. Since that season, I have worked primarily as a choreographer without a real base in the United States, keeping my repertory active by giving works to other companies. I was particularly fortunate to have been a part of the *Past/Forward* project of Mikhail Baryshnikov, which allowed me to revive works from the Judson era and to mount recent works on the dancers in his troupe. It has been a privilege to be active in different fields of the performing arts, continuing to work with Robert Wilson and to be involved with European dance and theater.

New York City
March 29, 2003

6
Meredith Monk (b. 1942)

Meredith Monk grew up on the East Coast in a musical family. Her early training in Dalcroze eurhythmics started her on her path of connecting music to movement, which has remained with her. After graduating in 1964 from Sarah Lawrence College, where she created a combined degree program that included music, dance, and theater, she headed to New York City and soon presented her work in galleries, churches, and other spaces, and became a pioneer of site-specific work. The House, the company she formed in 1968, has performed her work in lofts, museums, parking lots, fields, and theaters. In 1978 she created Meredith Monk & Vocal Ensemble. Monk's wide-ranging work—intimate solo vocal concerts, films, interdisciplinary theater pieces, and large-scale operas—have been presented worldwide. United States sites include the Houston Grand Opera, Carnegie Hall, the Guggenheim Museum, the Brooklyn Academy of Music, and the New York Film Festival.

Monk has pioneered the investigation of the human voice without words, exploring its many colors and movements and discovering haunting sounds previously unheard. Arising from her singing, her movement style tends toward understated, often repetitive gestures that suggest narrative and character without literally telling a story. Yet her operas and multiperceptual works have personas who live in spatial, kinetic, and imagistic landscapes that she pieces together like mosaics. Monk encourages her performers to bring their personal qualities to the work—their whimsy, energy, talents, and vulnerability. Her goal is to create an art with transformative power for both the performers and the audience. According to Monk, "Underlying the aspect of the interdisciplinary work…is the belief that one can weave together these elements and make a form that utilizes the whole human organism and all its perceptions."

Meredith Monk has been granted some of the highest honors available for her work, including the MacArthur "Genius" Award in 1995, two Guggenheim Fellowships, three Obies, a Bessie Award for Sustained Creative Achievement, the 1986 National Music Theater Award, sixteen ASCAP awards for musical composition, and honorary doctorates from the Juilliard School, the Boston Conservatory, the San Francisco Art Institute, and others. She has made over a dozen recordings of her music.

* * *

Meredith Monk (photo Massimo Agus)

Meredith Monk

I come from a musical family. My mother was a professional singer on the radio; my grandfather was a singer and ran a music conservatory; my great-grandfather was a cantor; and my grandmother, whom I never knew, was a concert pianist. I was singing melodies before I talked and reading music before I read words. In contrast, I was not terribly agile as a child and had trouble with simple coordinations like skipping and jumping, perhaps due to my inability to fuse two visual images together. My mother had heard about Dalcroze eurhythmics, which was being taught in Steinway Hall by two Polish sisters, Lola and Mita Rohm. I started studying Dalcroze when I was very young, around the age of three. It was a wonderful basis for both my music and my movement. A lot of children learn music through movement, but I was learning movement through music.

I didn't realize what a big influence Dalcroze was on my work until 1991, when I was working on my opera *ATLAS* for the Houston Grand Opera. The classical singers there come from a tradition of thinking in terms of long musical lines. They have a certain lyrical idea of singing and phrasing that is not rhythmically very articulated, so they were having a hard time hearing the larger cycles in my music, which is rhythmically complex. I remember their asking me, "How are you hearing this?" and I said, "I don't know, I just feel it. I have no problem. I can go way out and come right back around to the 'one' again." And they said, "It's because of your Dalcroze training that this is in your body." I was always able to sense somatic rhythms. I had the combination of having natural rhythm and being a natural musician and then coming across those amazing teachers.

Space was another big element in Dalcroze: movement in space and music in space. In their way of teaching *solfège*, when you sing a scale you move your arms up in space so that you get the concept of low to high. I work a lot with visual image, but music, movement, and space are really the essence of what I do. So for me Dalcroze was like finding home base at an early age. It was a strong influence that has persisted.

I have a very idiosyncratic body. For someone who is built the way I am and has a lot of technical problems by nature, I could name a million reasons why I could not be in Balanchine's company. But necessity is the mother of invention, so in a way my limitations became a kind of strength. I had to find my own style, my own way of thinking about movement, my own way of structuring in space.

When I was a student at Sarah Lawrence in the early sixties, I was trying to break down some of the directions that were being given to me. I was always interested in using the imagination rather than in using straight kinetic ideas like making a dance about falling. If we were assigned something like that, I figured out some way to subvert it. By my sophomore year, my style was already starting to form.

I was also finding my way vocally at that time. I sang *lieder* and was in the opera workshop; and I was playing guitar and singing to earn my way through college. But I realized that I didn't want to be an interpreter. I made a score for myself on tape that I danced to. I did a little bit of singing and dancing at the same time. That was a bare beginning of discovering that I wanted to combine movement and voice.

When I left Sarah Lawrence in 1964, I came to New York and was doing solos that consisted mainly of gestural movement and were very cinematic in nature. Asking myself how to make a solo that had cuts in it like a film led me to make *Break*, which was very fast and jagged. Since I'm short, I always had a lot of speed as a mover and could go from one state to another in one second. Making *Break* gave me the opportunity to explore quick shifts in energy, mood, and image. But I really missed singing, so I sat at the piano and started vocalizing and suddenly had a revelation: I could develop a vocabulary for my own voice in the same way that I had with my body. The voice could be gender and age and landscape. It could also be kinetic. What would a spiral be for the voice? Or jumping? Or falling? And because my vocal instrument was more virtuosic than my dance instrument, I had more to work with. But I could use the same kind of philosophy I used with movement. I've always been grateful that I had the choreography background in school, because I could apply some of the same principles to working with the voice.

As a creator, from the mid-sixties on, I gave up the conventional dance form in favor of a more inclusive interdisciplinary approach. Movement became one layer of a multiperceptual performance form including vocal music, visual images, and film. As far as my movement style was concerned, I began working on a more primordial way of moving that was not based on the balletic or Western tradition but much more based on the body in its honesty. A gesture-based movement emerged from my work with the voice. When I first did *Songs from the Hill*, I used to stand at the microphone and sing the pieces very quietly, just a microphone and me. But in the late seventies we were in Taormina, Italy, in a huge amphitheater. The acoustics were beautiful, so I was unmiked. But it was an audience of tourists expecting some gigantic production, like *Aida*, with elephants walking across that space. I just about had to be carried on. There I was, standing in the middle of that vast space like the sacrifice of the vestal virgin. The audience wasn't throwing things, but some of them were playing kazoos. To have a single person standing there singing was definitely not what they expected. Especially my kind of singing. So somehow, for survival's sake, I started incorporating gestures into the singing. And so it's as if the vocal aspects created this choreography, this gesture. It came out of the songs themselves. And now it's stayed there.

Basically my work is a big tree with two main branches. One branch is the exploration of the human voice as the original instrument, as a language that delineates energies for which we have no words. That branch has included a deep exploration of my own vocal instrument and what it can do. It's also included the work with my ensemble, making CDs, doing music concerts—all those forms that have to do with the voice itself.

And then the other main branch is what I call the combine forms, or the interdisciplinary forms, which are the big, live performance works, the musical theater works, the operas, and the films. Underlying the aspect of the interdisciplinary work—or what I think of as multiperceptual work—is the belief that one can weave together these elements and make a form that utilizes the whole human organism and all its perceptions. It's a holistic idea, very much an antidote to the fragmentation and specialization that we live with in our world. It dates all the way back to when I was in school at Sarah Lawrence and I needed to try to find some way of weaving together the different interests and talents I had had as a child. It was a way toward a kind of psychic health for me then and still is.

When I came to New York after college and was reading a lot of philosophy, I saw that Western European culture is the only one that sets up specialized categories. I realized that, in contrast, my personal impulse to tie together several artistic disciplines was an affirmation of the richness of the human organism: a microcosm of a much more universal awareness. If you think about African culture, a master drummer is also a master dancer, a master singer, and a master storyteller. In Indonesia, the more skills that one body has, the more that person is respected. Someone could be a great singer and a great musician and a great dancer. You are not jeopardized or penalized for that multiplicity the way you are here. Instead you are honored. That integration also existed in ancient theater forms. So my interdisciplinary idea was more aligned with these other cultures. I saw that my nonlinear form reflected the complexity of the contemporary world.

Even though I'm most interested in creating art that is timeless, I enjoy when my work speaks to the time in which I live or when the process of making a piece feels inevitable. *Quarry*, first shown in 1976, was like that.

It took over and became itself. *Facing North* in 1990 was also an effortless process. You always wish that it will be like that, but you can't have that expectation or then it surely won't happen.

For *Quarry* I began with an overall concept: to make a piece that was a meditation about World War II. So I did some research. For years I read and visited archives. But I knew I wanted to create a kind of abstract, poetic documentary. How do you deal with World War II in a way that's not covered by the media or by what we've been told about it? How do you evoke it as poetry? I was working on all the elements at the same time: the images, the music, some of the movement ideas, the characters, and the visual aspect. Also the space, the environmental aspect of it, the colors—everything simultaneously. When I was a young artist, I usually worked from an idea first and then filled in the materials. For example, in the mid- and late sixties, when I was interested in subverting conventional notions of time and space in a performance situation, I first chose my architectural or outdoor spaces and then let them inform the structure of the work. In *Juice* and *Vessel*, both of which took place in three different locations on three different days and dealt with memory, change of scale, and the literal act of traveling as part of the experience, I began with the overall vision and the material flowed from that.

These days, I'm continually making the "liquid" but don't always start with the container. Part of the process is hanging out in the unknown. With each form that I make, particularly the interdisciplinary forms, I'm excited that I don't know what the form is going to be when I start. That's where I find my energy and my passion. For *The Politics of Quiet* in 1996, I had the music when I went into rehearsal and I kept on trying to put images with it and the piece kept on saying, "No, no, no, I don't want theater, the music holds by itself." It did not want theatrical images and I had to live with that. The piece has movement elements, but very simple, no tricks visually. I had no idea what it would be until we finished and I realized, "Oh, this is something like an oratorio, an abstract, nonverbal oratorio form."

In *Magic Frequencies*, which was a piece that came after *The Politics of Quiet*, I was working more with the different elements at the same time, but I didn't have an overall concept to start out with as I did with *Quarry*. I just had some materials. I had music materials; I had visual materials; I had ideas. I didn't really have movement, but in rehearsal we started working on a little bit of movement. And I wasn't sure how the whole piece was going to fall together. Then I suddenly realized that it was going to be a science fiction piece. When I finally got the name *Magic Frequencies*, everything fell into place. In that piece, there's music all the way through, but it's not as complex as the music for *The Politics of Quiet*. So there's more balance between the music and the theatrical elements, which are very whimsical and rich. I feel that each piece demands a different kind of balance and you have to find out what it wants. Each of my pieces creates a kind of world and part of my job is to let that world come into being without my getting in the way. Another part of my job is to ask what the laws of this particular world are. And the piece answers it.

It's like making a soup. You have the vegetables for a while and they are what they are and then you put them into the pot and they start boiling. At a certain point you know that it's going to start getting to the essential soup. You have to wait until the time when the essence is ready to be put into its form. Then the structure comes in. If you try to structure too early, sometimes it doesn't work. You have to let everything simmer there for a while and be what it is before you realize what the piece really needs and what you can throw away.

If I look at an early piece like *16 Millimeter Earrings*, I think, "How did I do that at age twenty-three?" It looks like work that I would do now. Maybe I knew everything I had to know at the age of twenty-three. Maybe I haven't gone ahead at all. But I don't think of my work as a line. I always think of spirals or cycles. So it's more like the way clothing styles come back around again in a new way. When I look at that piece, I see it's a young woman's rite of passage, going from adolescence to adulthood. We have different parts of life where we can share our wisdom and our life's insights in one way or another. I feel that in some ways now my work is getting more transparent and things are actually falling away rather than getting bigger and bigger. Everything is getting more down to the bone and more pared away. Not smaller and smaller, but more essentialized.

You always know when your work is coming from your center, your core source, and you always know when it has come through you. That's when it feels like the grounding is right and then you can build off that. Sometimes whole pieces don't come through you, yet you still have to make the piece. But you just hope that there will be at least something in the piece that comes from that place of quiet. It's that place I seek rather than trying too hard and going through the motions. If you labor too hard it's like manufacturing a product. There are a lot of people who are product makers. I'm not. I'm a process person. I have an interest in actually getting to some level of truth and I hope the result will be of use to people. But it's not that I do product after product, that Meredith Monk always makes a certain kind of piece. If I did that I wouldn't grow. I need to take risks all the time. It can be very painful. But when I'm able to push ahead, something very exciting happens, even if it doesn't totally work.

Matisse is an inspiration to me. If you look at a retrospective of his work, you can see that for a period he would work on a new set of ideas. It could take five or six or seven paintings or ten paintings until you see: "Ah, it's locked in now; now he's found it." Then he might have done some more paintings in that realm, but not many. He would have moved on to the next exploration. That's more the way I work.

Unlike visual artists, we can't produce sketches. We have to make whole pieces. Our audiences have got to live through them too. But one thing that is so beautiful about live performance is that it's organic and it grows, like a child. And you're always changing and adjusting and finding out more about a piece as you perform it. The audience senses that we're in a precarious place. I think that level of vulnerability is very much appreciated by an audience. The Native Americans always leave a little hole in the basket; the Japanese leave one imperfection in a pot so that it has a kind of life.

I used to ask painters how they know when their work is done because I know that one extra stroke can ruin it. Live performance is so delicate you can change something and lose the magic. But you also have the chance to put it back a lot easier than painters do. I think that in working on live performance, a piece is never finished. You're always working on it, even if the form is close to what it should be. I always say to people that if they come opening night, they should come back three weeks later and they'll see a totally altered piece. I think having an audience is part of the work in a live performance form. Installation or film is different. If I make a movie, once I make that final cut on the negative, it's going to be pretty hard to change. I have to live with my mistakes. But in live performance that exchange of energy, the figure 8 of energy, is part of the work.

Structure has always been important to me. I don't want my structures to be too rigid. Yet they must be rigorous. It's a strange combination of rigor and freedom. I'm always looking at the whole, always interested in making the building brick by brick and still somehow figuring out how to ensure that there's air within it. Especially when I'm working with different layers and elements, I consider, "How can I weave these things together? How do I keep them as layers so that they become luminous against each other?"

I write big charts that have layers. Here are my music materials for instruments. Here are my music materials for voice. Here are my music materials for voice and instruments. Then here are my movement ideas. Here are my images. Here are my objects. Here are my lighting ideas. Here are my environmental ideas. Here are my costume ideas. Here are my color ideas.

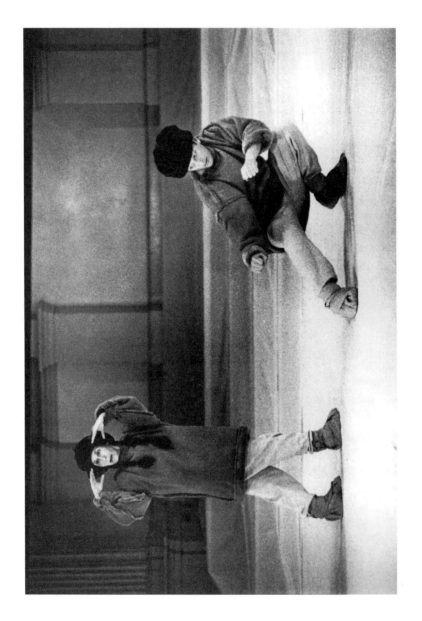

Meredith Monk and Robert Een in *Facing North* (photo Joyce George)

Magic Frequencies by Meredith Monk (photo Clemens Kalisher)

At a certain point I have to do a catalog: What do I have? At a certain point I have to do an order: What comes first? Sometimes I have index cards and a bulletin board and I put them in different kinds of grids, to see how things line up. On the top I might have music and then images and then objects and then video. The vertical dimension is the time line. I start lining them up and see how what I have fits in. It's like the way you edit a film. Yet overall the work is more like a mosaic.

In making a new piece, the first feeling is fear. It's terrifying to hang out in the unknown. But you go ahead anyway on blind faith. There's usually some point in the process where my interest and curiosity take over. For example, after I made *Book of Days* in the late eighties, people said, "How did you make a feature-length film with responsibility for a million dollar budget? Weren't you just terrified every day?" And I said, "No, actually I was too busy and interested to be scared." At a certain point your curiosity and interest and your immersion in the material take over and then the fear is not there any more. The end result is usually fairly satisfying and fulfilling. But there's also a kind of sadness because by then you've lost the early excitement in the potentiality of it. When you actually make the form you have to live with that.

The time between finishing a piece and starting the next one is always hard. It's a time of emptiness. I know people who start working on the next project right away but it can be to protect themselves from that feeling of emptiness. I'm never able to do that. The periods of emptiness are hard to bear but it's tolerating them that leads to your being able to make each piece be itself; you're not just going ahead with habitual behavior to protect yourself from these feelings.

There's a lot of waiting in this process. The visual artist Ann Hamilton and I collaborated on a new piece called *mercy*. Ann and I both are people who have to wait. I'm so glad she's here on this planet because there is somebody else who understands what torture it is to have to wait. I sit at the piano every day anyway, trying things out. I went for a whole month at the MacDowell Colony, sitting there day after day after day, and finally, on the last day, I got something I liked.

Making my work is a combination of a lot of solitude and then working with people. Philosophically, if I'm working with people who are going to be performing a piece of mine, I want them to know where the decision making is coming from and that their suggestions will be listened to. I want this process to be alive for them. If I'm just telling them what to do, it doesn't have that same level of commitment. I spend a lot of time alone before I go into rehearsal. Then I have a rehearsal period, then I spend a lot of time alone again. Some people imagine that we do free-for-all improvisation, but that's not the way we work at all. I don't go into rehearsal where we're just going to do an improvisation. I never know how to use material generated like that. I come in with a small parameter that I'm interested in, and then we can play with the material. There's a lot of room for play and I give total credit to the amazing creativity and intelligence and patience of my performers.

I've always spent long times with my groups. I can't just get a pickup company to learn how to do my kind of singing, so I've been working with a lot of the same people since *ATLAS*, for over ten years. We evolve a kind of shorthand to communicate among ourselves. It's a lot easier for me to work that way because I feel like they understand the basic vocabulary, and the basic philosophy as well. It's like a philosophy of life that you have to pass on. It's not just a matter of your singing this and your singing that. It's a way of thinking. And that takes a while to develop. One thing that's so courageous about these people is that they have to give up the instant gratification and ego fulfillment that some work offers. There's a renunciation in performing my work, which even I have to carry out as well. It's about always seeing the big whole and about immersing yourself in the material. In a sense you become transparent.

It takes a lot of courage to perform that way, to be so quiet about your performing and not use your habitual behavior to get attention and love. I think that if you're pushing forward or pulling back with your energy, the impulses that are genuine don't have room to come through. They're forced. We're trying to create a performance situation that's nonmanipulative. You're centered and people can feel that. The audience has a lot of space to experience transformation right in front of their eyes.

Someone like the Japanese Butoh artist Kazuo Ohno is an incredible inspiration. He's ninety-four years old. When you see his work, it is like you've just gone to church or temple. You've had an experience of pure love. I think I'm most interested in that kind of transcendent experience—if it's possible to make it happen within a performing context. Not that I don't want people to have a good time. Joy is certainly part of the experience. But what I try to offer is a full spectrum of feeling within one evening.

The process of making work has a lot in common with meditation practice. Both involve discipline, openness, immediacy, and focus. My meditation practice has helped me along in the "life" part of my life. The continual insight is fundamental because if you're not nurturing yourself as a person you end up not having much to say as an artist as the years go on.

My goal has always been to keep working until the day I die and to still be discovering. I think discovering is the only thing that keeps me going. You feel like you're part of something much bigger than yourself. It's worth all the effort. I've had a great life. I've seen the world through the work. It's been a kind of path.

I've been working almost forty years. After a while you find that you have to contend with the backpack of your past on a lot of levels. How do you find something new? How do you explore something you haven't done before? How do you keep it fresh? How do you challenge yourself? How do you risk? How do you do something that really has a lot of life energy in it? All that has a lot to do with trying to consider yourself as a human being first. As a youth, I was most interested in pursuing my art. My identity was defined by my work. But now I'm starting to learn that I'm also allowed to just be. That realization makes the work much less in need of an obvious kind of control and much more about vulnerability and compassion—which I think is the direction you have to go in as an older person. There are examples of artists who have armored themselves. They can end up becoming caricatures of themselves. That's one choice, to continue the fixation, the armoring, to maintain that defensive stance. I think the other side of it is to allow yourself to become soft and vulnerable. You have to pick yourself up all the time, but that becomes something that you can share with other people. Then I think the work has a lot more to say and its power is enduring.

East Meredith, New York
December 20, 2001

7

Elizabeth Streb (b. 1950)

Elizabeth Streb grew up in Rochester, New York, and graduated from the State University of New York (SUNY) at Brockport as a dance major in 1972. She performed for two years with Margaret Jenkins in San Francisco before moving to New York City, where, in 1975, she founded her company STREB/Ringside. Always questioning the dance world's assumptions about movement, Streb has incorporated the actions and values of the circus, rodeo, and daredevil stunts in her work. Over the years these moves have included dancers' diving off a sixteen-feet-high metal scaffolding (a "truss") and landing flat on a mat or hurling themselves through the air in quick succession with timing so precise that they just miss occupying the same space at the same time. Her work requires great physical strength, stamina, coordination, and daring. Wanting to better understand the effects of movement on matter, Streb is studying math, physics, and philosophy as a Dean's Special Scholar at New York University.

Over the years she has focused increasingly on single actions, notably falls and collisions in their myriad incarnations. Custom-made trapezes, trusses, trampolines, and even a flying machine give her the means for exploring bodies moving in space subject to gravity and other invisible forces. In recent years her presentations have become less stark than they once were, incorporating projections of slides, videos, and text. She now includes music as part of her show's ambiance, although she has always maintained that movement has its own timing, unrelated to music. Wanting to reach more than the usual dance audience, she has shown her work not only at high art venues such as Lincoln Center, the Spoleto Festival, and theaters worldwide, but in Grand Central Station and Coney Island in

New York and in the mall in front of the Smithsonian in Washington, D.C. Passionate in her desire to see everybody moving, she has recently established S.L.A.M. (Streb Laboratory for Action Movement), in Williamsburg, Brooklyn, with the door literally open for community people to come in and watch and take classes.

Streb is the recipient of a MacArthur "Genius" Award, two New York Dance and Performance (Bessie) Awards, and grants from the John Simon Guggenheim Foundation, the National Endowment for the Arts, the New York Foundation for the Arts, and the Mellon Foundation, among others. Her work has been featured on TV shows including *Alive from Off Center*, *World News Tonight*, and the *Late Show*.

* * *

Elizabeth Streb (photo Rose Eichenbaum)

Elizabeth Streb

I feel it's my mission on earth to make movement. I don't really question it. That's just always been true. When I was younger I did downhill skiing and motorcycle riding and sports. It was what I loved most and what took me to another place. When I went speeding down the hill, it was life to me, so I never had doubts.

I'm always thinking about movement. I don't think I was ever just a dancer. I was too curious, even while I was doing it, about all the mysteries of movement. And I certainly didn't think that all I was told was true. I remember in Margy Jenkins's class everyone would tell me to stop doing everything so muscularly. And I would think, "What if every move was initiated by the muscles instead of trying to just move the skeleton, what then? Why are you saying relax when it's hard? Why should we have no expression on the face and just pretend that it's easy? It's not. Why can't I push harder than I need to? Aren't the invisible forces of movement interesting? You can't touch them. But you can see them when they happen." The whole thing about efficiency, about never using more than you need to, I'd wonder, "Why shouldn't I? Why not perturb the air?" And so all the questions. Of course I was feeling a little defensive as a dance student. But the fact is I didn't want to move their way. And I couldn't get my silent responses out of my mind.

When you train as a dancer, you're hearing the history of people's opinions on how you should look. But I thought modern dance was all about figuring out your way to move in the world with your own unique piece of equipment. That's what Martha Graham and Isadora Duncan and maybe Ruth St. Denis and certainly Mary Wigman were all about. They all had peculiarities. And Merce Cunningham. All of this made me interested in modern dance, but not necessarily in what had happened thus far in modern dance. The Judson Dance Theater and the seventies for me were the most vibrant and interesting time: Yvonne Rainer and all those people. But after that, in the eighties and nineties, I became uninterested in most people's movement ideas.

When I first started making work I didn't know about the theater world. I was quite ignorant of it. I came from a working-class background and had never seen a show on stage until I went to college and saw Alwin Nikolais. I had seen the circus, which I just loved. I loved the way it smelled and I loved the minstrel life. I loved the carnival essence of the nameless people who risked their lives doing single movements over and over and over again. That's the holy calling of their life on a certain level. I was very attracted to these circus performers. I could either do that or I could go become a nun in a convent because I also loved the single idea of returning to monastic ritual. I never disliked Catholic school. I loved that they told us to take ninety-degree turns and be quiet and walk in single file. Although I wouldn't do it, I liked that we were supposed to. I liked the regimen and the discipline that the nuns imposed on us.

I think part of my advantage was that I was not from a wealthy family. I used to assist my father, who was a bricklayer. Nothing seemed hard to me after that. When I was maybe ten years old, I would go on the job with him and carry stone and buckets of water all day long from the lake. He'd say, "Go get a bucket of water." And I'd go down to the lake with two huge buckets. I'd scoop them up completely full and I'd walk all the way up to the foundation he was laying, and he'd say, "Dump 'em in there." And then I'd think, "I won't stop until he tells me he has enough water. If he says, 'Okay that's enough water,' I'll stop." I'd go back and forth all day long bringing the water up. He never did tell me to stop. It was like apprenticing to a madman. He built our house and our cottage. One day he said to me, "Hold that ceiling up 'cause I got to go get some more nails." It was heavy sheet rock. An hour later I was still there, waiting, saying to myself, "I don't really care about coming down off this ladder. I'll be here. I can be here forever. I don't care." Like him, I am a maniac, so my bar is pretty high for what you can handle and how little you can live on or what crazy scams you can do in order to be a dancer in New York City.

I did show a couple of solos in San Francisco in the early seventies, but they were almost old-fashioned, modern dance, expressionistic pieces because I was trained in Limón and Humphrey-Weidman technique by Susannah Newman Payton, Irma Pylyshenko, and Jim Payton at SUNY Brockport. That was my movement base. I'd performed for Margy Jenkins and for Molissa Fenley and other innovators in downtown New York. But I didn't understand doing dance steps. I didn't understand why that was interesting to watch. I understood why it was interesting to do, at least for some people, but not to watch. I found when I started studying Cunningham and ballet that I wasn't comfortable doing the normal vocabulary. And I missed velocity. I got my physical information from my downhill skiing from age ten to twenty-four and from driving a motorcycle. So my proclivities led to a particular carved-out zone of interest having to do with extreme issues of action. It requires impact; it requires velocity; it requires manufacturing not just ideas but those conditions.

In 1981 I wanted to see what would happen if gravity was altered at a tilt of forty degrees and what would happen to the body if it went up and down that slope for half an hour. So when I first made *Fall Line* for Dance Theater Workshop, I built a hill to work with. I remember thinking, "Oh my God, they'll never let me get this thing in there, you know, seven hundred pounds." It was outrageous. And there were the pole dances in which I tossed and caught some long poles and stepped over and around them, and moved in ways the poles helped to define. And I did a piece just about being on the floor and using that as a place to be, never getting up. I started thinking about unhabitual places in space. I figured that if you didn't feel like you were physically uncomfortable, then you were in a cliché-ridden universe. So I developed situations to get into what people normally call discomfort or pain, but my company and I have called "rather interesting physical sensations."

I choreograph because I have to. Movement has always been the only thing I'm interested in. Or if not the only thing, certainly the most passionate thing that draws my attention. And it's not only *people* moving that attracts me. It can be machinery moving; it can be animals; or just theoretical ideas about movement. I think movement plays an ultimate role in our world. It's the ultimate attention-getter. You're having a conversation with someone really interesting on the street and some erratic motion happens in view. Immediately your attention goes to the movement. I also think it's an outlawed, transgressive activity. I hear invectives by parents all the time in airports: "Sit down and sit still. Stop moving." Kids are told over and over and over again not to move. I think that movement of any sort is taught out of young people year by year, gradually and effectively, to the point where people get more and more withdrawn from the physical world and from themselves as physical bodies. So I try to up the ante and to design events that, while inserted into an artificial space, are real and effective actions that people can reattach to; it touches their memory banks somehow. It is my intention that the viewers will understand, that they will have an experience that is physical by their witnessing it. That's my goal. And I guess that's about as good as it gets.

I'm starting more and more to think of myself as a founder of this way of asking questions about movement. But just a founder because, while I certainly bring my drawing book to rehearsals to get us going, there's no question that I also count on the skill bank of the dancers, their sets of questions, their reasons for being there; I don't want a bunch of robots. These guys are "thinking movers" in every imaginable way. I'm honored to have every one of these people here. I want to figure out how to plumb that part of it. That's why two of Terry Dean Bartlett's pieces, *Spin* and *Gravity*, are in the show. His pieces are going to manifest these questions differently. That's how movement hands itself off as the years go on. I'm trying to figure out in a company situation how to embrace that and to make sure that the dancers have a major influence over my ultimate decisions and what you see on stage. But I don't ask them to create material that I then manipulate like some choreographers do.

During rehearsal periods we rehearse five hours a day. I don't give a company class, so they usually go to a class or the gym before they come, which means they have about a seven-hour day. I've never wanted to be a teacher, but some of the newer dancers have never had any of my instruction, so I do a ten-minute technique enhancer at the beginning of each rehearsal with them. I see what's weak or what might need to be more deeply explained, like right now it's the why and wherefore of hitting each other in the air. Both the conceptual idea and how we can work toward it. That's how the rehearsal begins.

There are certain moves we're getting to that are new places for me and I'm finding that there is a resistance among the dancers. There are certain ideas that I approach that they don't want to do. If I mention the idea of impact in the air, they clear to the edges of the room. So we haven't gone very far with that idea. We've landed on hard ground that doesn't move and on a ball and on slanted surfaces; we've flown through the air and done parabolic flight and all of that; but we've never hit something that then moves, an unstable impact surface. It's actually a very difficult technique to work on—because it's a stupid thing to do. And there's no way to legislate how to do it. It's a technique that's somewhere out there. A few years ago I tried it and then abandoned it because I thought there's just so much you can ask people to do. And you don't want to hurt dancers. They have to do this as a career.

And then there's the dance called *Squirm* with all eight of them stacked in a locked transparent box and then one more squirms through. It was very, very hard to work on that. They'd really go mad when they all got in there. Until they figured out exactly how to stack, the bottom guy, Eli, was yelling, "Get off, get off!" Sometimes I could only work on that five minutes a day. It was a very interesting place to be. And horrible. Brian, the one who squirms up the front, is claustrophobic. And I said, "Listen, I don't want you in the piece if you're claustrophobic." But then he really wanted to do it. I said, "If you're interested in why this is frightening for you and you want to trek into that territory, then let's go. We'll do it very slowly and then we'll back up and then go there again." So I felt excited about those two places because they were new for me. Especially now that I'm not performing, the dancers are my barometer. *I'm* not smacking into someone in the air.

The first response to my work is that I'm going too far. The dive through the sheet of glass in *Breakthru*—they said that's stupid. But I think if you keep going and you keep a perfect line, the move shows the effect of action on substance. If you can't show the effect of action on substance, then you don't really understand action completely. Those three pieces—the impact, the box, and the dive—are about going to a place that's not comfortable and that actually you've been told is off limits. Especially when they close the box and then lock it, it's "Wait a minute, get me out of here!" For a good month I was completely startled by the reaction of audiences, which was pretty vociferous. I didn't understand that it wasn't just a zany, weird thing. It had some kind of resonance for people in their lives, like, "Oh, my God, don't do that, please!"

Or how about inverted swings as you're being hoisted up by a cord? Your head hanging down is so vulnerable. And you're on this little cord and you're not in a position where it would be okay if the cord broke. You're just holding a perfect line anyway. Those are just emblematic ideas. The one I really want to do would be called *Tip and Fall*. You'd be more than thirty feet up on the truss; you'd tip; you'd be tied by your ankles, and you'd fall headfirst and land two inches from the ground. Now, technically, I can't do that, though I still want to. But no rigger in the world will guarantee that kind of stunt.

The piece called *Bounce* is done on a piece of gymnastic flooring set in the middle of the performance space. My first idea for *Bounce* was that somebody could do a front tuck flip and somebody else could dive through the center of their flip. I just got that image in my head. I thought, "Well, that hollow space is negative space. Why can't somebody just watch one person's flip over and over and over and see the consistency of the space they leave and when it's available for them to pass through?" We never yet have accomplished that because the curled-up person's head occupies part of the enclosed space—and always a different part throughout the duration of the flip. I still think it would be possible.

The concept I ended up using for *Bounce* is similar, though. The dancers are placed around an eight-feet square sprung mat. To start, the dancers in turn hurl themselves onto the mat, understanding, however, that there's no room for their body in the space they're aiming for because somebody's already there. But they go anyway—and the person who's there has to be gone by the time the next person lands. So it's occupation and deoccupation, occupation and deoccupation of that limited space. Or one dancer takes the high road horizontally through the air and another takes the low road and maybe they can have enough propulsion to just miss each other when they land. And then tens and tens of crossings occur; and then a couple of times we'd just not leave the mat and have people land on each other to demonstrate how close the timing had to be for such a small area and eight people to keep traversing it properly: I'm here, I'm here, I'm here, I'm here, I'm here, I'm here. Can you move that fast? It had to do with taking the entire body, not one part of it, and getting it on and off a particular place in space extremely rapidly. Reflexively. Without having to transfer weight to get off. And then to have many of these moments happen over and over and over again.

That piece got built in one-second chunks. We would work on the solo moves. Even once they're set, the moves start to disintegrate if we don't attend to them. I need to go back to clarify: It's not that she's on the ground and then you land on her. You're in the air facing stomach down; she's in the air facing up. Neither of you has landed. Then you're over each other and you both land. It's an anti-intuitive thing to do. You tend not to want to do that. Your faces will smack into each other—which has happened. People have gotten split lips and nose cracks. But it can be done if you're in a perfect line and at the same time you land flush, in a way that you could never have prescribed. It's a process of discovery.

I have not changed *Bounce* because I think it is what it is and I think it's still good enough to be in the show. But everything else I've changed. I get bored and I cut sections out or I make them shorter. I question why we are still doing this or that. Right now there are about twenty "moments" in the show. Everything is getting shorter.

Usually my questions start spatially. What information is specific to a given place in space? We live in places that have fairly static boundaries, and therefore we minimize the actual nature of space. But space is complicated. Think about mathematical topography. I'm wearing a Moebius strip ring. Okay, think of a strip of paper. It has two sides. You can connect it to make a ring. But if you first twist it 180 degrees and then connect it, you find that when you follow the surface around, it is all one side. And one edge. Okay, I rest my case about the outrageousness of space. If we could figure out what that warp means in terms of movement and occupying space, it would be profound. My point is that my company tries sometimes with contraptions and sometimes in other ways to reiterate space as it exists. I think that when what we do is specific and true to space, it resounds with the audience.

I'm also particularly interested in vertical surfaces and so I made the wall pieces. People think this new wall piece is the same wall piece I did in 1991, just because I'm using a wall. If you use the same old pirouette turn, is that the same old dance? You're on the ground, on your feet, right side up. Why isn't that the same dance? I just happen to use a vertical surface. They see it and think, "Oh, the wall dance." Well, thanks for not noticing any of the vocabulary. Okay, I do a couple of the moves that are part of our vernacular. But so do you in normal dance! It's as though I must never do that move again. So I recalibrate how I use the wall. In one piece we show the wall upstage with the dancers coming at it from downstage. In *EDGE*, we use a plexiglass wall that is more downstage so that the audience sees the dancers' bodies coming toward them and actually contacting the wall through the transparent surface.

For the bungee piece, I collaborated with the Espana brothers, Ivan and Noe Espana. They're from a five-generation circus family. We worked on the piece in Grand Central Station for a month this summer. The pragmatics are not separate from the creative part. Getting the truss in there took a week longer than it was supposed to, etcetera. I won't go into the bloody story of all the technical stuff required by having this much equipment. But you need to put the attaching in-point for a bungee at thirty-two feet. So the structure that was built was determined by what types of actions I wanted to do. I would like to have two months of just working on the bungees. I'd add catchers. We'd expand the trajectories. We'd get the timing down. Right now, okay, it's a vertical piece, but it's still just emblematic. I need time spent with the sixteen- to thirty-two-foot space. I feel like the first sixteen feet off the earth's surface is fine. I get it. But I want to go higher. That's the hunk of space that I'm interested in. But to get that costs $10,000 a month for rehearsal space.

In a lot of what I do, I get information from what the equipment is able to do. Then I'll sit with my drawing book and draw out a story board. It's pretty explicit. I'll take those templates into the rehearsal studio and teach the moves to the dancers.

The trampoline work that we did for *Up* started with the single idea of isolating the direction up. I thought of the high area as an underemphasized theatrical space. We bought a trampoline in Australia. When we got the trampoline into the studio we realized that even just to stay vertical on it was impossible because there's so much force. And when you land, your ground is curved. That experience was alarming. I usually try to make sure I have a good enough idea to work with before I get the equipment, which is so expensive. But when I got the trampoline in 1995 and we were experimenting with it in my studio on Canal Street, I was thinking, "This is really $3,000 down the drain. This is not going to work." Then, little by little by little, people were able to do duets on the bed. And then actual vocabulary.

We added pipes above the dancers that they could catch hold of, to mitigate the consistency and repetition of the up and down. The next problem was changing the base and size of the body's support: from your shins to your back to your stomach to your feet to your thigh to your upper back. And the different sound that made and the different move it initiated next. So it was a complicated process to gain the skills we wanted and then to put all the parts together. Of course, "up" isn't really clear unless there's "down." Or "stay" or "over" or "out." As the exploration gets more elaborate, it ends up with the cart driving the horse a lot of the time.

It's all about a physical event that's so peculiar to itself that you cannot prerecognize it. You're fishing. I think that's the most honest way for me to work. I am not a master of any particular form. I'm just seeing if I can create a condition, draw a design that will plumb new information. In turn, the information will resonate in a particular way for people watching us even though they themselves don't move.

When we had a residency at the Brooklyn Bridge Anchorage in 1993 I built a huge wall. It was always open to the public while we were working. And from that moment on I have had a program that I call "Public Access," which is about never working in private but always working with witnesses. Like Shakespeare's groundlings, the observers in the pit. You really don't know what you're doing when you're hermetically sealed. My new motto is "Interrupt the artist." When I was at Grand Central trying to work, I looked over my shoulder and I saw Ruby Lerner from Creative Capital, the group that had come to our rescue and been fabulous friends and funders. She said, "I didn't want to interrupt you," and I said, "Get over it. You can interrupt me." Construction workers are putting up buildings that cannot fall down. They get interrupted all the time. That has to be at least as important as our making this dance. If it's a good enough idea, I'll come back to it. My rudder at this point is so deep that I want to be interrupted. It makes the process more vibrant when I get interrupted. So I play into the idea that every little bit of human issue can come in and affect the decisions that I make and then get read by the public. I need to know if what I'm making is relevant. I get to know by being public. I love being alone and working on a problem and solving the problem alone, but I work in public. That's my job as an artist, as a person who has a 501C3, responsible to a not-for-profit organization that is publicly funded. It's my responsibility to be in public. But the art world wants you to work in private the way our cultural icons do. I hate all of that. It's like these bastions of culture that you pretend are going to be in a neighborhood.

Bilevel by Elizabeth Streb (photo Sandra DeSando)

Kitty Hawk by Elizabeth Streb (photo Aaron Henderson)

I used to go into the deli a block from the Brooklyn Academy of Music and ask, "Where's BAM?" The response was, "What? I don't know." And so I called someone in a high position at BAM, and told him, "By the way, your deli down there, they don't know who you are. You're failing at your job." I think it's the wrong way to work. I made a commitment to myself that in the future I'd check out that the people within a ten-block radius knew we were in their neighborhood.

I'm definitely interested in an audience that will tell me the truth about what I'm doing, so I have to appeal to people who aren't in my club, the art world. Of course, I'm really interested in creating a language that comes out of an investigative, theoretical, experimental downtown dance world. But then, rather than just constructing and deconstructing sets of languages for twenty years, I'm now setting myself a challenge to use the language in a way that's readable to any targeted audience. It's my job to find out how big my audience is now. I'm not going to accept that it's as big as the art world wants it to be, because I think the art world is effete and it's skeptical and it's also prejudiced and elitist. I think all those things from having participated in it. I'm also a guilty party. So part of my job as a social encounterer is to change that and to see how I want to operate outside this mold and to ask what is my civic duty as an artist working in the USA.

We worked for a month last summer in Grand Central Station. We didn't do lights or video there, thank God, because it really would have broken the bank. But I didn't want there to be no image at all, so I brought my friend's slide projector and I took slides from years and years ago and projected them in a tape loop on the wall. I really loved it because it was like the history of my company Ringside: when I was doing my poles, when we were at the Brooklyn Bridge Anchorage performance space, and then some other weird slides including zany swimmers in the air, like Leni Riefenstall's Olympics. The slide show just kept going, on the side.

Recently, I've been thinking that to interact with the audience, one of the things I would do would be like what Savion Glover did at the Variety Arts Center. There everyone knew that if they brought their tap shoes, at the end of the show there'd be a circle of light and the audience would go on up and do their own tap dancing. For us, at the beginning of our show, we could take our slide carousels out to the audience and collect their slides. Ours would be mixed up with theirs. The slides would be projected during the whole show, like a tape loop. And it would be their action moments, our action moments, action in general. I like that idea. I have to write that down.

For years I'd see other people's work and I'd think, "They use music, I wonder why. Does our idea of grace have something to do with the fact that they all use music? What happens if, instead of phrased sounds and transitions, we try out physical issues and transitions?" And I came to find out that with real physicality the transitions are quite abrupt. For instance, if you end a move five feet in the air and let gravity do the rest, you're going to have abrupt collisions when they land. Lo and behold, people saw that as violent and brutal. I saw it as the truth about movement. And the fact was that it happened because I set my actions to a time code that was not of the musical world but of the physical world. I didn't want to use someone else's map for my road when they're not going where I'm going.

The fact that I'm including music now has more to do with the show that I'm staging than with my investigations. I've come to believe after twenty years that people who walk into a show will not be happy if you do not tell them a story and they do not hear music. Actually, even I want those two elements. So I decided to stop this particular conversation: "Why isn't there music?" and "What's it about?" If after twenty years those questions still are the main two that resound, then let me just put in a couple of moments of music and stop that problem. It doesn't change the way I work, it just changes the fact that maybe people in the audience can relax.

How do you get uninitiated people to notice your language? I've found, because the language is so brutal—and there's no way to mitigate that—that there's a point at which they start to disbelieve that we're human; we start to turn into cartoon characters, and they get exhausted and hammered by the brutality or the intensity of it. So we have what I call sherbet moments, like *Air Swim* with the reflective mirrors and the Esther Williams music. I wanted to see if I could make a sequence that looked like it was under water but was on the ground. But I also wanted a sherbet moment in the show. "Okay, we're not going to be slamming now." The audience is thinking, "Oh, phew, thank God." So then we could come back and have them notice the actual moves again.

Since I've included music, text, and video, the reviews have been so interesting, really so great. I thought, "Jeez, why didn't I do this sooner?" They seem relieved that now they can talk about the work against this other environment, that I'm not forcing my aesthetic on the world in the way that I had been. It's a theatrical production. It's a graceful thing to do. I certainly put in my time not being graceful. One review called it "Streb multi-media event hits the stage." I like the idea of having all the different formats present. I think that, in the world, people receive information in all the ways that we use: text, simulated image, speech, action, color, and the visual. I question the idea, in live and time-based shows, of having only a singular discipline occurring. I'm not sure that movement alone can fill out a theatrical space in this day and age or keep people's attention in the way that I think a show needs to. So I am theatricalizing my show. However, I never put something in unless I'm attached to it in some way. Sometimes that's good and sometimes that's bad, and I need to know which is which. I have a cadre of friends who tell me the truth and I ask my agent to tell me the truth.

Our enterprise has gotten so expensive that the time that I can spend just working on choreography is much less than it was when I was younger and poorer and had less overhead. But I'm constantly making drawings and scribbling down ideas about what would be a great piece. Right now my body of work is a sequence of singularities. It's just single moves. It began with the dive through the glass. I think actions are often more effective when they're singular, and that, in fact, it is the essence of movement: to be a single move. If you design a moment in time, space, and body and it is a "right moment," that's it, that's everything. You're falling from thirty feet flat on your face. And what can that say about movement? About the world? About me? About you? If I were to pick a few single moments that are archetypal, what would those moments be?

I'm working up to jumping off vertically from the top of the truss. And then just start to run. The truss is twenty-five feet high. Since I just had a knee operation, I may never be able to do that, but I think a human *could* do that. When I make drawings now, it's with the idea of the ultimate show in mind. I'm thinking about a seventy-minute event with no intermission. So I just take a bit here, a bit there. I want there to be a little story. I want there to be some fire. I want there to be water. I want elements to be in the show.

I'm a New Yorker. I would never live anywhere else. I have an idea about having a show in Las Vegas, but I would want a couple of years in New York to build it and to have an extended run. Then I'd probably have to go out to Las Vegas for a good part of a year to set it up. And I'm going to talk to both John Coles and Ken Feld about that. Ken Feld, of Ringling Brothers, Barnum and Bailey, would want thirty people in the show. He even said he wants an elephant. I have an idea for an elephant, called *Stand*. Four people would be on stage, standing in a rectangle. The elephant would be off in the wings. You could see its little trunk come out. The elephant would be with a trainer. Then these four people would fall back as the elephant started to walk toward them. The elephant would walk between them, then the elephant trainer would go, "Hup." And the elephant would spring in one move and stand on the four bodies. Culturally, it's a comment on how for ages humans stood on elephants. What do you think? I'm so into it. I feel like everybody would understand it. I know it's weird. Well, you don't know until you try, right? There'd only be a quarter of the weight of the elephant on each person. That's why I'd want him to jump. Like, whhhp, suck over like that. Right now that's a fantasy dance.

I feel like something's got its hand on my head in a serious way, and it's the economy. How to get funding. Philanthropy could be a whole other conversation. Why don't they ever capitalize a show that comes out of the art world? So I've been thinking about going into a more popular performance world. And then a whole bunch of people say, "Oh, you're going to be ruined if you go with Ken Feld to Las Vegas," or "Aren't you worried about what your work will turn into?" And you know when I come back with, "Okay, name three examples of someone who sold out and ruined their work," of course nobody can because it's never happened. The myth is so absurd.

One of my big projects, which I don't necessarily consider an arty project but an inventive and creative one, is how can I get out of the ghetto? Can I get across the canyon? Can I figure out a way to prove my point that there's a huge audience for the arts out there? I've performed in fancy theaters all over the world. That was my goal five years ago. I dreamt about it. But it's not my goal any more. If I can be an example and cross that great chasm—if somebody would just give me a few million dollars and some professional guidance—I think it would be liberating. I'm impassioned about diversifying the audience. I think we would have huge audiences. There are six billion people in the world after all.

Philadelphia, Pennsylvania
November 3, 2000

8
Eiko Otake (b. 1952)

Eiko Otake was born in Japan and was a law and political science student when she decided to leave the university. She went to study with Tatsumi Hijikata and soon thereafter with Kazuo Ohno, two originators of Butoh (the avant-garde dance form devised in postwar Japan that taps ancient, primordial roots and tends toward dark and intense imagery). At Hijikata's studio Eiko met her partner and future husband, Koma Otake, with whom she has choreographed and performed ever since. In 1972 Eiko and Koma left Japan and traveled together to Europe where they studied with German expressionist dancer Manja Chmiel, further nourishing the stark, imagistic source of their dancing. They came to America in 1976 and stayed.

Eiko and Koma prefer to let their work define itself without reference to traditional or contemporary Japanese or European theatrical forms. An exploration of what they call "delicious movement," rather than the practice of any dance technique, underlies their work. Their dances are landscapes of the slowest possible movement, illuminating imperceptibly shifting images. Their movement takes place within sets and lighting of their own design, worlds engulfed in sand or snow or within the hollow of a constructed tree trunk. Swathed in fabric or nude, their bodies sculpt the space and become one with their surroundings. Eiko and Koma have also designed pieces for outdoor environments: rivers, beaches, and parks, and for performance in traveling caravan stages. They consider themselves performers above all, creating work that lives by sensing the responses of their audience. Their recent piece, *Offering*, which has toured extensively to outdoor sites with no admission fee, coincided with the disaster of

September 11, 2001, and humanity's response to it and has brought them full circle to their activist roots.

Eiko and Koma have received grants from the John Simon Guggenheim Foundation, the Mellon and Rockefeller Foundations, the Japan-United States Friendship Commission, the National Endowment for the Arts, and the New York State Council on the Arts, among many others. They are recipients of two New York Dance and Performance (Bessie) Awards and were honored with a MacArthur "Genius" Award.

* * *

Eiko in *Offering* by Eiko and Koma (photo Kathleen O'Donnell)

Eiko Otake

I was born in 1952 and Koma was born in 1948, so we didn't experience the war— except that when we were small, Japan was poor and felt like a part of the third world. It was not the country it is now. We didn't grow up with a refrigerator, TV, or washing machine. It's not that our families were particularly poor; the society itself was like that. Every night people would go to public bathhouses, where the kids as much as twelve years old would run around naked between the men's room and the women's room, where grown-ups were busy talking in a big bathtub or washing each other's backs. It was a different body culture and people were not yet compartmentalized into small families. We had much more street life. People told stories and played catch with hand-sewn gloves. That kind of community life affected Koma and me.

Because Japan is an island, we had never been invaded or governed by another country's power—before 1945. Japan had been closed for nearly 250 years, from the seventeenth century through the nineteenth century. Only one port was kept open, so knowledge and technology trickled in slowly, which gave ample time for the Japanese to find their own way of doing everything: technology, culture, and art. Being isolated made Japan a country that had time to invest in itself. As a result, Japan as a culture has developed a certain aesthetic, not because people there are more inclined to create beauty, but because they were given those particular circumstances.

During my great-grandparents' generation Japan was forced to open up after the isolation that spanned three centuries. With the new Meiji era in the late nineteenth and early twentieth centuries, the Japanese saw Western technologies and thoughts rushing in, yet they also retained the traditional culture and feudalistic values. Japanese intellectuals and artists since that time have had to deal with contrasting values and practices between two cultures that pulled and pushed. Then our defeat in World War II added a kind of chaos to Japanese society. Even though Koma and I were brought up in a postwar "democratic" Japan and didn't come from particularly traditional families, I realize now that, as Japanese, we breathed in certain visuals, certain stories, certain shadows, certain conflicts, and certain cultural enforcements without ever even being aware of it, which then fed into our aesthetic and thinking.

Thus both traditional culture and the chaos and new development of postwar Japan were influential for us. But so was the sixties counterculture. Koma and I were student fighters in an anti-Vietnam War/anti-establishment movement when we were political science university students. We were politicized and rebellious—which is why we left the university.

We did not want to serve the system that we detested. Without yet knowing each other, we each left and went separately to the studio of one of the originators of Butoh, Tatsumi Hijikata, where we met. Altogether Koma was there for six months and I was there for three months, certainly not long enough to identify ourselves as Hijikata's disciples. Hijikata's students were living in his studio and he let us dance right away in the performances. So those months, however short, were intense. After that we went to the great master Kazuo Ohno, who turned out to be our primary teacher. But we were still very politicized and questioned anything that had to do with a director or too great a person. We were against hierarchies and have never been interested in a disciple-teacher relationship, so we left his studio after a year to go to Europe.

Kazuo Ohno had become one of the most respected figures in the counterculture movement because his dance was a radical departure from anything previously done in Japan. He was an enduring figure, not a young man fighting for the sake of fighting. He carried deep passion within him that was ignited by seeing great performers: the Spanish dancer la Argentina, the German expressionist dancer Harald Kreutzberg, and the ballerina Anna Pavlova. Ohno was a religious person and studied very hard. Although he was very serious about his art, the way he presented himself was warm, even mild. He was very different from our generation, which was aggressive and loud in our questions and accusations—to the point of exhaustion. So we got to know this amazing person who was very different from, for example, a theater director whose motivation would just be to make a new piece. Ohno turned out to be a controversial figure not because he wanted to make that kind of impression but because of the person he inherently was. There is a huge difference in that.

We always joke that we are the worst students he ever had, but in a sense he put us in a special place because, although we left early, we kept in touch. On his first visit to New York, we produced his concert in a small loft. Since then he has performed maybe six different seasons here. Every time he would come we would drive him around and make food, so we'd have a strong family relationship. We saw him last month when we performed in Tokyo. He had come a long way and was in a wheelchair. We were crying. It seems like every time Koma and I are just about not to continue dancing—because we are still politicized and asking ourselves, "What are we doing? Should we be doing something else?"—we happen to see Ohno in a festival or he comes to New York to perform. Then he flares us up again.

When we left him in 1972, we went to Germany and studied with Manja Chmiel, who is eighty-two years old now. She worked with Mary Wigman for thirty years and was an acclaimed solo performer in Berlin.

At that point in our lives, Koma and I had not thought of marrying or making a lasting partnership. Our intention was to work together for a short time before we would go our separate ways. But when Manja saw our performance, she said, "You really have to stay together. Something is happening between you two." So we stayed together a little longer. It didn't matter to us if we separated then or three years from then. It was all an experiment. We did not know that this was the beginning of what is now thirty years of working and living together. After about a year, Manja said to us, "You mustn't remain here. You've got to go somewhere else, even though I'll always be here and I'll always be your teacher." So she sent us to Amsterdam and there we met Lucas Hoving who used to dance with José Limón. We're very lucky because, although we have never been serious students, we've had a way of making friends with our teachers, who were amazing people.

Lucas happened to have just come back from New York to become the head of the dance academy in Amsterdam. He said, "You can't stay here. You have to go to New York," and told us all about New York. Then I said, "Where do we perform if we go there?" He said, "Don't ask me that. Just get there. There are zillions of places to perform. It's not like I write you a recommendation, that there has to be one place. You just get there." There we were, two Japanese who had left our country and gone out completely on our own. If we hadn't met those people we would have been just young adventurers with absolutely no background or destiny. We were thoughtless and fearless. Those people saw something in us and encouraged us to continue to work together.

So Koma and I came to New York in 1976 on a six-month visa. I was only twenty-four years old. We had one prearranged engagement at the Japan Society. We performed there—to a small audience. Well, nobody knew us, so we gave away tickets to people who were in a nearby restaurant, hoping some people might come. Jack Anderson was in the audience for the first performance. He wrote quite a wonderful review in *Dance Magazine*, and within half a year—this really shows what the seventies were—we had performed in Dance Theater Workshop, Cubiculo, the Performance Garage, Donnell Library, the Lincoln Center Library, and San Francisco. By the time our six months were up, we had quite wonderful reviews from newspapers and we were filing for the next visa, which allowed us to stay longer. After that, with our friends' help, we applied for green cards. It was a rolling process. We didn't really plan to stay; we just came to see what would happen. The friends we made here made all the difference. They did so much for us: They found an apartment; they filed the official papers; they produced our show; they helped us tour. It was amazing. When you are young, you know little and may also be arrogant, so you tend to take for granted when people help you. I felt like we were in the process of an adventure and everybody was involved. But now I look back and I understand what extraordinary support our friends offered us.

Koma is an amazing man who comes up with crazy ideas that I couldn't do myself. He's the one who said, "Let's work with Anna Halprin," and got us going on our recent collaboration with her. He's the one who came up with the idea of making a traveling caravan piece with a custom-ordered trailer. But then sometimes I am the one who conceptualizes the idea, for example, in working out the titles. It's one thing to perform a piece with rice and call it *Rice*. Then it's just rice itself. But if you call it *Grain* and make the relationship to the food chain, it becomes more universal, it grounds us. Some people eat corn; other people eat wheat; we eat rice. All those cultures have a myth in relationship to where the food comes from, how dead bodies are buried, and how new life grows out of them. Their myths worldwide have a lot in common. I like that.

Koma works on the sets and does more of the heavy-duty labor because he is visual and strong, but both of us paint the sets, make costumes, and design the lighting. We take turns working on the many elements that constitute a piece. Then we check on each other's experiments and trials because we can bring a fresh view to what the other has done. I never make Koma's costume and he never makes mine because costumes have to fit and they have to have the right tears in the right places. I make my movement; Koma makes his. We comment. Sometimes we don't listen to each other, but I think we listen in our hearts. The duet part is hardest because we have to work things out between us. We improvise and we get each other's feedback. Then we improvise on top of what we have and get each other's feedback again. We have been working together for so long that certain decisions we can just make, but in certain areas we keep arguing and trying. The controversy helps us. In the process we are obliged to see each other's ideas and experiments. Then we come to a communal decision.

In coming up with movement, we ask, "Does it look right? Does it feel right?" It's a combination. For me, it has to hit a balance between how I feel kinetically and how it comes across to the audience visually and spiritually. If it feels wonderful but doesn't look like anything of significance, why bother? I have to be careful about not pleasing myself as a performer only; I want to please myself as an audience, too. The best way is to have good friends looking and commenting on works-in-progress. Or I imagine myself in an audience chair so that in my mind's eye I can see the dance and how it feels to me as a viewer. Sometimes we can do a piece that doesn't look like much but somehow delivers the spiritual concept. Certain choices also come out of the performances. We can do new things in performance and then feel them out a little bit afterward: Oh, this didn't work out or that did.

Especially because I live with Koma and we work together, our lives and work are intensely connected. In many ways all of our life experiences come from being performing artists. Almost every friend I have was made through our working. We go places; we meet people; then what we encounter in our life comes back to the dances, though not in the practical sense of bringing back a specific event from a specific day.

It's more about all those little reinforcements. Sometimes going down the street you notice a little flower shop or the mailbox that the next door neighbors have painted. Sometimes you decide to ignore it; sometimes you invest yourself in seeing. Rather than getting from place A to place B in a hurry, you can recognize the detail you encounter and enjoy it in the process. I think that's what we try to do ourselves through dancing and what we try to teach. When our children were performing with us there was a part where they had to walk very slowly. I used to tell them, "Don't think of looking far away. Think of looking toward Japan." You know, "far away" is an abstraction. But when you say, "Look toward Japan," you have to think about getting to California first, then about passing over the ocean, and then about the way you see Japan in your mind's eye. There's more nuanced detail. The gaze will have an inherent movement recognizing different entities rather than a straight line. I think we invest all of our life knowledge through that kind of nuance.

We made a piece called *Tree*. Potentially we could have made the same piece even if we had lost all our individual memories of the last twenty years because the piece is based upon a much longer time span. We try to get to a more unconscious level of memory than what we may personally remember or think about a particular tree.

We read books that relate to what we are working on, not because we put that knowledge directly into a dance, but because investigating the ideas gets us further interested in the subject we are to dance about. Right now I am studying atomic bomb literature. That probably has nothing to do with what we may be creating in the near future; but in the long run, I can't say that it won't find a way into our dance. Everything we do potentially feeds the work.

In midcareer we were very active as performers because we were inexpensive, we were small, and we were different. It meant that for each piece we created we had a long period of time during which we could perform and feel the piece out. But because it's such an extended process, sometimes we forget where it started. Eventually we get too used to the theme and structure, so then we begin to make changes on the piece. Since it's only the two of us, it is easy for us to do that. Sometimes we talk about it in advance; other times one of us makes a change in performance and the other has to accommodate. But then we may start to feel that a piece is getting broken down too much. The excitement of the performance carries it, but if we try too many new things within a piece, then the basic reason, the structure that formed the piece, the concept, suffers.

We may be the only ones who notice it, but after the performance we might start to argue: "Koma, why did you do that? You really are destroying that particular section." As a performer he wants to do it. But from the point of view of the choreography there's a conflict. So that's when we feel like starting a new piece—because we need a new venue to think about what we want to do as performers. For example, the piece called *Land*, a collaboration with Native American musicians, is influenced by the dry landscape of New Mexico. Performing it is physically abrasive because we grate our skin against the rough surface of the set. We get tired. Although we wanted to have something dry like that, we also ended up making a contrasting section because performing the abrasive section was just too much. It also led to our making a new piece, *Wind*, because after performing *Land* for a while we wanted to be a bit more airy.

It often takes about two years for us to make a full evening–length work. That's a long time to work on a piece, so there's plenty of zigzag in what we're thinking about and trying out. We have lots of arguments and lots of experiments. In an evening-length piece, unless we have something to come back to that grounds us, we can get lost. So it is crucial for us to have a title. We take titles very seriously. If we called a piece *Opus 13*, we could do almost anything we want, but we wouldn't have the concept to refer back to and see that certain material is wrong here. So we make a title as a serious attempt at getting grounded and a place for an audience to share our intentions and also bring in their own reflections. And we have a policy that every title that we perform is internationally understandable. It has to be easy English and really speak about the concept of the piece. And once the title is made, we do experiments with that concept. Koma does some movement; I do some movement; then we look at each other and identify that what we've done belongs to a particular concept, that it has a certain weight. That's how we determine the sections and the movement. We show the work in progress to see if it's practicable.

We started using sets with *Grain* in 1983. *Grain* had only a futon that we carried with us on the road and then a platform as well. The set was attainable any place we went. In contrast, *Passage* from 1990 was very set heavy. We had a whole environment with dripping water. Around that time we became interested in creating a visual space because that also anchors us. We became choreographers who were not making pieces necessarily for the movement's sake. Instead of first choosing the movement, we started by creating environments in which we exist; then the behavior pattern became almost self-determined. If we made a big tree as an environment, then what happens in front of the tree or in it is not so much about moving the arm at a forty-five-degree angle. It's more about how we relate to the tree.

When we create a piece for the theater, we take images from real life, then construct a set that will get put in the theater. When we are in an outdoor environment, everything is already there. Of course we still have to construct the concept of the performance because we are not just ordinary people living there that particular day. We have to put a condensed concept out there.

In *River* we perform in a shallow body of water. In preparation for the premier in 1995 we worked every day in a small stream in the Catskills. It took literally a whole month to know what we wanted to do with the river and to figure out the light and the movement. We got really cold working in the water. After our premier, the second performance was done three weeks later in the Delaware, which is a big river. But there we only needed one week to prepare because we already had the concept, a flowchart, and nicknames for each section. The sections had to be visually reworked, but that was much easier. We don't want to be so site specific that, after taking one year to make a piece, we do only two performances and then it's over. We want to be much more flexible than that because we need to tour; this is how we make a living. We also think that performing the same work in different incarnations strengthens the concept of a piece. We like to make the core of the design so that if you see our *River* performance in the Catskills and your friend sees it in Delaware, you can actually talk about your experience and feel that you have seen the same piece in terms of the basic concept.

River has a simple flowchart: Everything comes from upstream and goes downstream. The audience gathers on the riverbank about when the sun sets. The scenery by the river is active: birds, bats, fish, clouds, boats, neighboring sounds. They have plenty to see and hear before we appear. Koma comes from upstream floating with the driftwood. He surrenders to the flow sometimes and at other times resists. That becomes a dance. Then I join the river as Koma floats downstream with the driftwood as far as he can be seen.

I dance with the river, its water, its flow, its reflection, and its sound. Whenever I surrender to the flow, I get carried a little way by the current. The natural light changes rapidly at that time of the day and soon it is twilight. As the sky gets darker the primitive lighting we set up gains in intensity. The surroundings become less particular and soon I am dancing in the black mass of water, the most ancient river, the ancestor of all rivers. Koma disappears around the bend, sneaks out of the river, bicycles upstream, unseen by the audience. Local kids often spot him with his wet costume on his bike. When he floats from upstream again and joins me, it is as if Koma has now been reincarnated. Then, joining with the driftwood, one continues downstream, then the other follows. Really, we're just repeating the fact that we are always coming from the past and going to the future. We are being born and we're dying. We keep floating downstream. The people who are watching us floating down the river look all the way downstream until they can't see us any longer. Then they are back to seeing their own river, but we hope now with its ancient continuity. There is so much life going on there; it always has been and it will be. I think the audience feels our point.

Once we have that flowchart with simple props and lighting plan, then we can adapt the piece wherever we go. When we perform in a lake, depending on the landscape and where the sun sets, we decide which direction is upstream, which is downstream, and the rest follows. Sometimes we have to reel the driftwood along to create the movement of flow. That part is adjustable. Other than that, we have the piece. There's always a specialness to each place, but we don't want to come to each new place without a plan.

The landscape in our work is not a literal study from nature. We also see the living body as a possible landscape. We don't necessarily distinguish between a human's body, an animal's body, a stone's body, and the mountain. The body is moving; the mountain is also moving. The mountain is resting; the body is resting. *Night Tide*, one of our favorite pieces that has stayed in our repertoire the longest, came from the period when we were living in the Catskills in the early eighties. We would go outside in the night and at first couldn't see because it was so dark. Eventually our eyes would get adjusted. The longer we stayed outside, the more we could see; we even could start to see movement in the trees and the landscape. We began to think about the mountains and how in Japan certain mountains could have a female name and certain mountains have a male character. Sometimes we actually had a story to base the work on and sometimes we decided we *could* make up those stories, like the mountains making love in the middle of the night when no one is looking.

*The **Caravan Project*** by Eiko and Koma (photo Tom Brazil)

River by Eiko and Koma (photo Tom Brazil)

Night Tide, which we premiered in 1984, was the first piece we performed naked. For that reason it was controversial. The piece itself has nothing controversial in it. It's really just bodies coming up from the floor and going down, then rolling toward each other. Then it's, "Oh, morning is coming. We have to go back so that people don't notice we can move and make love." It's a simple piece. We really couldn't add any more dance movement and still stay true to the original idea. We didn't originally intend to be naked; we just didn't have a good costume to wear that would make sense. Performing naked was both a liberation and a challenge. We said, "A fish is naked and a stone is naked. Why not us?" We can forget sometimes we are humans. It was the honest thing. For that reason, that short piece is significant to us.

We still perform *Night Tide*. We recently performed it in Tokyo. We also performed a piece called *Snow* in the same program, which is a romantic love duet. But if we did two pieces that are all costumed and both beautiful, then we'd feel like it's just not us. We need to reveal something and we need to present ourselves as vulnerable. I don't want the whole evening to be about showing beautiful movement in beautiful costumes. We like to have a balance.

We developed the extreme slow movement because slow movement reads well with nudity. A body then becomes an emotive landscape. Because we were not wearing costumes the movement became a little more selective. For aesthetic reasons, once you are naked, you are not jumping up and down. We're not required to jump around anyhow for the concept of pieces such as "tree" or "rust." We didn't want to be seen merely as human nude bodies. I didn't want to be seen as Eiko Otake, a thirty-six-year-old Japanese woman at the time. That's too personal. We wanted to be transformed. We wanted to stay within the feeling of the dance. Now I can also be costumed and do slow movement because I am better in tune with the feelings, the sense of shape, and the sense of body mass.

In our relationship to composers and collaborators, Koma and I both come up with an idea, but I am often the one to write and talk about them. I happen to be a little more verbal, and Koma is a little more physical and visual, so there's a natural division. Just like in a publishing house, we have different departments.

We work only with people we want to spend time with, to eat and drink with. Each time it's different. We collaborated with the composer Somei Sato and the Kronos Quartet. We did not know Somei's music, but somebody introduced us to it and we found it very beautiful. When I reached him, he said, "Well, Kronos would be great for my music." So I felt obliged at least to call—"My composer said you are the ultimate"—and it turned out they wanted to do it. I never would have thought about working with Kronos unless something of that odd nature had happened.

The last piece we did at the Brooklyn Academy of Music, *When Nights Were Dark*, was a collaboration with gospel singers. We went to many different churches, on and on, trying to find gospel groups. No group wanted to do it, so we had to find individuals who did. Our composer, Joseph Jennings, who is African-American, went with us wandering the streets, where we eventually found people. Then one thing led to another. It was organic.

There are no set rules. It's not that I don't examine their résumés. We come up with a choice one way or another but we never work with someone just because they're well known. Our collaboration becomes humanly invested because we like each other. It's also risky for that reason. So far we've done really well in that all the collaborations have been learning experiences and have also brought us deep friendship and tribal trust which stay with us after the project is done. Working on *Land* with Robert Mirabal and Reynold Lujan, both Native American musicians from Taos: The four of us really thought hard about the land at Taos and at Hiroshima. Then *Be With* was created with our long-time friends Anna Halprin and Joan Jeanrenaud. Deep friendship doesn't mean the process may not have difficult times. But I think it is important that we start with a good trust so we can have our difficult conversations without ending or twisting the relationship. We want collaboration in its true sense and we really do collaborate from the beginning until the end. But we do it only when we can afford it, mentally and timewise. Since we don't collaborate often, I look forward to it each time with deep excitement. It's nice when all of a sudden we're not talking about an Eiko and Koma piece but are talking about a larger "we." Eiko and Koma have been talking about Eiko and Koma for so long it feels self-absorbed, whereas if we talk about our work with Anna and Joan, it's a different entity. It makes me feel honestly proud because it's all of us working together and each of us owns a part. I like that a lot. That is where the title *Be With* comes from.

We have also worked with our children in performance. They were so small and so beautiful because they were young and at that age everybody is beautiful. I'm glad we did that together because they now know what the theater involves. I told our children that there are no "mistakes" on stage because whatever happens becomes a reality. We are such a small company; we work closely with the local crew. Being in the theater the whole day, we get friendly with the people working there. It is important to us to feel that relationship, the communal work. Our children have seen the way we work. They know that we speak about difficult issues and argue; they also see the cooperation. It really is teamwork in the theater. It's not a lonely art.

The show *Breath* that we did at the Whitney Museum in 1998 was another sort of milestone because we performed it seven to eight hours a day for an entire month. We were there when the museum opened each day and we were there until the museum closed. It was unthinkable. It wasn't our idea. When the Whitney commissioned us to create an installation, I thought, "Great, they were now acknowledging our set-making aesthetic." Yes, they said, the set was beautiful—but beautiful in relationship to what we do. And the curator was right: Our set making, our environment is special really in relationship to the human body.

They said we could be present in the installation at certain times, like two, three, and four o'clock in the afternoon, and they would post the time so that people would know when to come. It sounded like feeding time at the zoo and we didn't want to do that. So we decided we'd just be there all day. Fortunately, it turned out it was not necessary for the two of us to be in it all the time because people were not there to see an Eiko and Koma dance. Most of the time we took turns, which was nice because then I could see it from the outside, which I never had before. People would just wander in without any expectations. It even took them a while to realize there was a human in the set piece.

We've never done anything like that before. It really took courage. It was a big experiment but I'm glad we did it. We were able to be more involved in completing the work visually without concern for a beginning, middle, and end, like in a theater piece. So many people came back to see us again that we felt our bodies to be accountable during that month as part of a larger city landscape—a part that was living, breathing, never still.

That experience gave us much more courage to take our work out to where theater rules do not apply. So we created a series of outdoor works that we perform in a park or a community garden. We realized people could come for five minutes or stay for the whole piece. Even five minutes could be worthwhile. You don't have to understand it or see a conclusion. If you see a picture by a painter, you don't have to look at it for an hour to appreciate the beauty. Since then, when we do *The Caravan Project*—for which we transport a small set in a modified trailer—some places we stay and perform one hour and some places we perform three hours continuously. Where we stay three hours we don't expect people to remain the entire time. We deliver our art and people come and go, just like they would gather around an ice cream truck, buy ice cream, find their friends, and talk to each other. It takes on the sense of a summer gathering place, which we like. The museum piece gave us permission to think about people coming and staying as long as they want and then leaving whenever they want to; it was liberating. If some are there more than a minute, it's their choice to be there, rather than their being more or less obliged to stay, as they are in a theater.

Often when we perform in the theater, tickets are expensive, and, although we don't tailor the work to the audience, we feel we are responsible to give something—whether or not they like what we give. We have been so lucky, performing at sophisticated venues in many wonderful cities. But the people who come to sophisticated places are the people who are often privileged and culturally well educated. They're a wonderful audience and I think it is important for us to have that audience. But in the meantime we want to know what our work could mean to the people who are not used to coming to the theater. In *The Caravan Project*, all we need to provide is five minutes' worth of what we do. And since we don't know when that five minutes will happen for each person, it's given us a different sense of performance. Instead of serving a climax, each passage and each moment becomes essentially important like no other.

Sometimes in a performance I can feel the audience energy, and that becomes part of my experience. If I linger too long I might feel that their energy fades away. Not to say that I'm making a logical dialogue, but there's an organic connection that may not even be conscious. We are not entertainers but neither do we want to torture people. We just are trying to be more elemental and true to our own taste, even though for some it may also turn out to be controversial. We're not looking at society and trying to come up with a big message that is controversial. We don't do that.

In making a new piece, as soon as we know the basic vision, how the set looks, maybe the lighting, the environment, and what we are wearing, then I feel better. Like with cooking, your past experience tells you that once you have the right ingredients, you can make something that may satisfy. Nonetheless, the first few performances are usually quite a mess. We used to feel all the time, "Oh, what we did was terrible," because our aim was high and the reality was low and we were suffering from the difference. As you get older, not only don't you aim as high, because you become realistic, but you also realize that it's not fair to the audience to disparage what you've done. They see what they see and we don't really have a right to speak for them. Once we perform it, we should at least believe that there was something there. Sometimes if we don't get to believe in it, we pretend we believe in it—because that is the easiest way to *come to* believe in it.

I teach my dance classes that way: Pretend you feel great. In fact you want your students to feel genuinely connected, but you can't get them there by saying, "Please genuinely connect." So I tell them about my two children and how when they were small they would say that they couldn't sleep. You can't really put them to sleep. If you say, "Yes you can sleep if you count a hundred sheep," then of course they say, "I already counted a hundred sheep and I still can't sleep." But if you say, "You don't have to sleep; you can just pretend you're asleep," then it won't take long before they fall asleep. It worked for my children and it usually works for the students because it's the easiest way to be in a particular form, in a particular movement, in a particular environment. After the class, they have the rest of their lifetime to make the material their own if they wish.

We, too, sometimes need to think this way. When I first performed *Offering*, no matter how much I rehearsed it, I was not comfortable. We lie on a mound of dirt and twigs. The dirt is dirty and it's hard and it's hot. We get injured. I had to pretend that I was comfortable so that I could actually get to feel the piece. I used the fact that all these people were watching and—even though I was not comfortable, even though I didn't feel like doing the piece—my job was to pretend I was at peace. It's not a lie. It is a device that better prepares one's body and stance. Once I can make believe I am there for the audience, I can work better. We are able to bring in the audience's mind to help us out. My mind can reside between my body and the audience's eyes.

Koma and I really are not choreographers. We don't have good training. I can count on my fingers the times we've choreographed for other people. We really are performers. The choreography is only the preparation to perform. Each performance becomes the work. I look forward to our performance, which elevates and transforms me. I appreciate that abstraction. We've been doing this work a long time and should be able to do it even when we're not ready. Of course we try to be as ready as possible, but it's a different feeling from trying to make a piece of art that is stunning and perfect. Because we started to present our work so early, we never felt we were worthy to make a breathtaking work or a big statement. We started before we knew what we had. I appreciate that because otherwise we would never have been able to do the work.

By now we have been working for a long time, so we have built a relationship with an audience. Of course nobody sees all our work. But certain people see a few pieces so they make a line of connection. If you read one piece by J. D. Salinger, then you are connected to that piece. But if you read several pieces then you can start to see the line of that writer and you have a more powerful relationship with their work. If you start to see several works by an artist, then you have a better chance of also seeing their line and what it intersects and what it runs parallel to. We are trying to create this line, not necessarily one great piece. I feel clear about that. We're not the kind of artists who perfect and perfect and perfect and then go on to perform. But there's a certain ingredient that allows people who keep coming to our performances to see what we are thinking in the long run. It's a kind of continuity, a kind of commitment, a kind of thinking that an artist delivers. This is the kind of relationship with an audience that I'm interested in.

Almost every piece is the last piece. It's very dramatic with us. We thought that way even when we were young, but then we still had our future and could imagine many interesting projects to do either together or separately. Now we're getting older, so while we still tend to feel this to be our last piece, we're not as courageously inspired to say what else we would do instead. We must think about our survival, too.

Until we get tired of the most recent piece we really don't have any desire to make a new one. We have many good pieces that really haven't toured a lot, so, in a sense, there's not much reason to make a new one unless we really want to. But then, somehow, I don't know why, we find we have already started. And once you start, you regret it, but by the time you regret it, you've invested too much in it, so you almost have to finish it. Then you pride yourself on finishing it. One thing leads to another.

In our current project, our sense of activism and adventure is taking over our choreography. I feel very charged right now in reaction to our out-door, free performances of *Offering*. You'd think that a free performance would be easier to attend, but I've noticed that it actually is more difficult. It doesn't cost the audience any money but it costs them more commit-ment. I really like that. The money exchange is easy to deal with. They already are familiar with a culture of spending as a way to budget their time and money. They make reservations, find a friend to go with, make dinner plans. Here we're creating a new pattern of thinking and behavior. In Seattle last month we performed along the beach, so the audience had a long walk from their cars and it was hard for them to find us. People had to ask themselves, "Do I really want to go? Maybe it's too cold tonight." But the fact is that once they got there they had invested themselves. They were bundled up against the cold. We too were cold, but the collaboration of the audience made the work possible. I felt very high in Seattle because the audience also made an effort. In making *Offering*, we had been aware the relationship with the audience would be different, but we didn't *feel* that difference until the performances. The reality of the interaction outdid my expectation.

After the Seattle performance we had to drive through the night to get to Portland. At the park in Portland where we performed, there is a beautiful fountain that fills with water and then empties every five minutes. A very beautiful flow and ebb. Even though *Offering* was made to be done on dirt, we decided to branch out from the original concept. We changed our costumes to fur, which could get wet, and used water and candles. Doing this performance on the second anniversary of September 11, we realized that dirt would have fit with trouble and burials, but water could bring cleansing. We didn't plan to do it this way, but we were willing to forgo something that we had choreographed and to change the point. That's not choreography; it's executing an event with a concept. You can do that only when you are absolutely comfortable with your concept, so you can break down the surface and have trust.

This project is giving us an opportunity to experiment more than to choreograph. If you are the choreographer who can do only what you prepared, then you get defeated when things are not the way you expect them to be. But if you come into the process as an experimentalist, the more different it is, the more exciting it is. This is our life's work right now.

New York City
October 18, 2002, and October 3, 2003

9
Bill T. Jones (b. 1952)

Bill T. Jones was the tenth of twelve children in a migrant family that settled in the small upstate town of Wayland, New York. In the 1970s he attended the State University of New York (SUNY) at Binghamton, where he studied ballet and modern dance and met his partner, the photographer Arnie Zane. They connected with Lois Welk through a contact improvisation workshop she taught at SUNY Brockport and went on to work together as the American Dance Asylum in Binghamton. Jones and Zane began making duets that drew on Jones's supple physicality and Zane's visual acuity. Their pieces played off their shared intimacy and striking physical contrasts: black and white, tall and short, fluid and jagged. In 1976 Jones started to show his work in New York City, and in 1978 he and Zane moved to be near the city. They formed the Bill T. Jones/Arnie Zane Dance Company in 1982, which Jones has continued to direct since Zane's death in 1988.

Bill T. Jones has made dances with strong political messages, using talking and décor to help represent the underrepresented: gays, blacks, those with HIV/AIDS, and others facing death. In addition to being an activist and storyteller, Jones has increasingly focused on structuring beautifully crafted group dances. In them he combines his mastery at improvising lush, complex phrases with his desire to explore music, time, space, and movement. Jones's work ranges from confrontational to tender, intuitive to formal, narrative to abstract. His work is animated by his own commandingly athletic and theatrical presence on stage and his ability to evoke a strong commitment from his company members.

Bill T. Jones is the recipient of a *Dance Magazine* Award, the MacArthur "Genius" Award, three New York Dance and Performance (Bessie) Awards, and choreographic fellowships from the National Endowment for the Arts. The Dance Heritage Coalition has named him an Irreplaceable Dance Treasure. His work has been seen on PBS's *Great Performances, Alive from Off Center,* and *Dance in America.* He has received honorary doctorates from the Art Institute of Chicago, Bard College, the Juilliard School, and Swarthmore College. Bill T. Jones is the author of *Last Night on Earth* and, with Arnie Zane, *Body against Body.*

* * *

Bill T. Jones (photo Susan Kuklin)

Bill T. Jones

I danced because I fell in love with my sweat. But I wanted a type of sweat that was not the sweat of the athletic field or the locker room. I wanted a poetic sweat. I didn't know what that was. I was nineteen. I wanted to be great; I wanted to be beautiful; I wanted to be loved. And I loved what my body would say to me when I was dancing.

Then I saw the work of Martha Graham. I saw the work of some other important people, not all of them dancers, and I began to think, "How can I aspire to this? How can I participate in this dialogue that has been going on?" And the first way was dancing for myself, with the scrutiny of teachers, then finding a like-minded community of young people who didn't know much more than I did, and we began to dance with and for each other. And, before you knew it, there was a thing called a career.

When we were in college at SUNY at Binghamton, Arnie Zane and I were part of a cool elite, all those groovy, postminimalist artists, the poetic folks, the nonnarrative folks. We didn't see ourselves as involved in the mainstream at all. As a matter of fact, that is why we did not want to be in New York. New York was a place we called Babylon, where any serious persons would lose their souls. But after making a series of rather brash works in the 1980s, works that were trying to combine high and low culture, Arnie and I did find ourselves in New York.

Arnie died in 1988. Up until that time I thought of myself as a member of a celebrated interracial, homosexual duet. Now one member had died. So who and what was I then? A big question. I wanted to understand what it meant to have a black voice. I wanted to find a way that I could now come out as a man who was 360 degrees, all of my experiences. And 360 degrees meant that I had to be able to speak to the fact that I come from migrant workers, the fact that I am a big fan of Eurocentric art, the fact that my lover was a Jewish-Italian homosexual man, and the fact that we had decided that we were going to live this life differently from our working-class background.

All of this stuff was to be shown in a large work that was called *Last Supper at Uncle Tom's Cabin/The Promised Land*, which was first performed in 1990. I had to go back and ask myself, "What did my heart understand about my mother's religion?" On Christmas morning my mother would pray until she was limp, sweating, totally in a state of ecstasy. To a five-year-old, it was a very important thing to see. A lot of my work was about trying to get back to that place. I also had to ask myself, "What was the relationship of Martin Luther King's 'I have a dream' to the gay liberation struggle? If there *was* a relationship." Both my mother and King were looking toward a promised land. For me the promised land would be a world that I would aspire to, that would be different from this one. And so the last image in the dance stopped being art and became an act of faith. A stage full of fifty-two-plus people, black, white, Hispanic, old, young, rich, poor, gay, straight, Republican, Democrat, what have you. All naked on stage bathed in a golden light and singing like children.

The next work was going to deal even more profoundly with what all people have in common. It was going to start with the idea of mortality as the thing that unites us: the fact that we are born, we must develop, and then we must die. It was going to be a work that needed the help of other people. I'm HIV positive—something that I have known since 1985, three years before Arnie died. *Still/Here*, from 1994, used the process of doing workshops that were called "dancing and moving about life and death." Of the hundred or so people who took this series of workshops, 30 percent were women with breast cancer. The lowest percentage was people with HIV. I said to all of them, "I'm not a practitioner; I'm not a doctor; I'm not a therapist. I'm not here to make you feel good. I need information. How do you get up every day? How do you live? How do you go to bed? How do you dare fall in love with anyone? How do you dare have a child if you're unsure about your life?" I said, "Tell me how. You know something. I am an artist and I am a man. The artist wants you to tell your stories in a way that makes me want to sing and dance. The man needs his hand held."

In developing *Still/Here*, media artist Gretchen Bender and I traveled around the country. We visited about thirty-five cities, where we video-taped workshops in which the participants made movement. They talked me through the story of their lives. Those tapes were given to Vernon Reid and Ken Frazelle, who made them into a musical score. With my company, we took the arm gestures that the people had made and we put compli-cated leg movements to them. True, the piece was a big and sprawling thing, but it was certainly not asking for anyone's sympathy. I said to these survivor workshop participants, "Help me make something so that people can learn not to be so scared about the conditions of our being here, which is that we are born and we must die."

After that, since about 1995, I've wanted to go back and understand more about movement. The other stuff, life and death, would be forever. As my mother would say, it's as true as the color of my face. That's never going to change. But what could I affect? The output of my company. Creating movement. Finding my style of movement. My taste. Maybe the purpose of engagement in this life of art and ideas is to develop a taste. Once you have figured out what you're doing, what it should look like, smell like, sound like, well, then you do that. You do it probably better and better, finer and finer. But then there's this question about how to keep what the Zen Buddhists call "fresh mind." How to keep fresh mind when you know your taste? Dangerous! The issues change over one's lifetime. Artists who are in their eighties are not the same as artists who are in their thirties. But I bet any one of those artists in their eighties has got to have a way to ask the questions anew.

Every night during my piece *Verbum* when the Orion Quartet plays the third movement of the Beethoven String Quartet in F Major—and it is a transcendental movement—I listen. How do they do it every night? As an improviser who came from the sloppy sixties, I can get to those supreme places *sometimes*. But they can get there *every time*. Now, does my wish to be able to do that make me a conservative old fart? I don't know. That's another one of my spiritual struggles.

I want my dancers to be in a place of engagement with themselves and their dancing. I wish to put into young people early on a sense of discipline and the sense that they are involved in something that is a spiritual pursuit. You must approach it like any serious spiritual pursuit with a form that we call a practice. Respect your body, which is your instrument. Understand it. Understand its boundaries, its history, how it fits into the world. Make sure you're equipped with intellectual curiosity so that you can answer questions about what you do. And keep a healthy emotional life. How multidimensional are you? What do you care about? How does your understanding of the world and your place in it manifest itself in your actions?

I used to say that *who* people *were* in the work was more important than *what* they were *doing*. Now I feel almost the opposite. And that runs the risk of using my company purely as bodies, except that I'm constantly asking them, "What are you thinking?" When people joined my company, I used to say, "Watch yourself, you're precious. Are you married? Are you in a relationship? Why are you dancing? Why?" I'd nail them to the wall with questions about their opinions and thoughts. Rehearsals would stop and we would discuss things.

The work I was doing was very personal. Then I'd give it to the company. There are places where I'd give them an image of some sentimental thing my mother had said to me. "Okay, if that image is not going to work for you, what *is* going to do it for you? There must be an urgency in it. What are you feeling at any moment in this abstract work?" And then I'd say to them, "I can tell when you're lying." And I'm constantly in their faces. "You're being lazy. You're hiding. You're not putting anything in here. I can tell. I can tell."

They'd ask, "But what do you want from us? We're doing the movement!"

"Well, what do *you* want from the movement? Why are you doing something that's meaningless?"

"Well, I don't know, tell me what it means."

"No," I'd say, "it has to be in *you*. Give it meaning."

And I'd pin them down in the training too. What is the truth of dropping the arm? The arm has weight. Don't fake the drop. Can you taste what a real drop of the arm is? I can tell if you're faking, if you're pushing the arm down. No, it has to drop, at will. You have to know what gravity is. Now, can you drop the arm on the beat of three? Can you listen to your breath and your muscles so closely that on the count of three you can access the drop? And that defines a kind of spirituality. How to be in the animal body, subject to the laws of gravity, the air, and now to use those elemental things as a painter, as a musician, at will, because you have done the work. Now that's called a "style." A style that has its own logic. I'm just beginning to try to build a style.

Keeping a company intact is a big challenge in a world where you can change a channel at any moment. I don't like people who change companies very much. I say to the dancers, "You know, this is not about coming in and getting the steps, right? There's an investment here. Do you want to be here? There are a lot of places you could be. 'Cause if you're here, Bill T. Jones is going to be in your face all the time." Then something is invested. There's anger, tears, all sorts of stuff. The stuff that life is made of. That's what art is supposed to be showing us how to do, right?

I'm glad to say that several dancers stayed with me for ten years. I think the greater proportion of them averages maybe four or five years. It's amazing how fast the time passes. And there are some people who are only there for two years. *D-Man in the Waters* was made in 1988 in its first incarnation and has continued; it never really left the repertory. Without exaggerating, maybe seventy-five people have come through that piece. Personalities who have had to learn it and take it up.

I'm a good dancer and I can get a lot of colors and reveal many states of mind and feelings in a series of movements. I can shift quickly from one state to another. Oftentimes the reason for the changes is that a lot of rocket-fire emotional propositions are piling up on each other. Their jostling together yields an unusual phrase. Now, you take away Bill's internal life and what is the phrase made out of? That's a big question. I make good movement when I make it on my body. I'm a persuasive dancer in the moment. Now I'm trying to become stronger at translating it for the company, at managing the grand palette. Twelve dancers moving together on stage is difficult. Exciting when it works, but difficult to achieve—particularly when I'm so interested in details, little wiggles, strange non sequiturs, different facings, and so on. Organizing the whole company in space is what I call the architecture of the stage. Balanchine—one of my heroes—could make the big palette appear inevitable. But I don't want to be quite so obviously architectural. It's got to be a little looser because I want to sense its flow rather than its lines.

I want to find a way to put this raw movement on stage and make it mean something. The universe is a messy place. The situation of being a human being is messy and crazy. It's hard to know much about it. Can you have a system of art making that can take on your hunches and produce something? To make that happen, the work has to have a fire inside of it. I know that we don't all have a shared meaning. But even though I don't believe that everyone will ever agree on anything, I keep making dances with the ideal, with the faith, that the audience is going to be drawn into it, be moved by it, or at least connect to it.

Oftentimes a dance is a feeling state in its nascent incarnation. And sometimes a dance arises from a really good improvisation wherein I'm relaxed or loose and everything is falling into place. There are propositions coming from both my mind and my muscles; and these propositions are persuasive and rich. I follow them and something comes out that makes me think, "Whoa! Where did that come from?" And if I'm lucky, there was a video camera on.

I often do set up the video camera. In viewing the tape afterward, I think, "Now here, what an interesting thing. What was it? Why did I do that? Why did I do that following that?" And that process is rich; it is the doorway for me into a dance company life, for, as I say, I'm developing a style. What is a style? Well, how do you dance, Bill? What is special in your dancing? What is personal? Then, looking at the tape, I can see it because it was coming almost unmediated, coming out of me. That's a wonderful place to be.

When I improvise, I put on Beethoven, I put on Mozart, whatever the assignment. I have to listen to it and think just as I used to think when I'd stand in front of the jukebox in our living room when I was about ten or twelve years old and was dancing to that other music. Hearing the Beethoven, I try to find a groove. I try to remember James Brown on *The Ed Sullivan Show*. I try to remember what the hips felt like in pop movement. I am definitely James Brown and my mother's prayers; all that stuff is in the muscles and bones. But whose language am I speaking? As Toni

Morrison says, "The black folks are the first postmodernists." By defini-
tion, we're already deconstructing a language that's been given to us. How
to use it? How to arrange it? How to inflect it? If that's not postmodern,
what is?

The last movement of the Beethoven, *Es muss sein*, for my new dance
Verbum, is made of two improvisations that were done all in a piece one
hot afternoon in Paris. I knew the music and was scared to death of it
because of its counterpoint, its rhythm, and its speed. But I put on the tape
and I said, "Okay, go!" And I recorded two improvisations on video. They
were eight minutes each. You've got to have the stamina and the ideas. I'm
a pretty good improviser. As I move, motifs get proposed and then later
returned to and developed. They might not be the final and most appropriate manifestation when it's freshly improvised, but at least the drawing
is there. Now, oftentimes when I'm improvising, I will do a leg movement
that indicates something much more virtuosic than I'm able to do. I'll say,
"But this is not for me. This is for the women in the company with free
hips." Such a movement is like a signal for myself. It has its own kind of
integrity and is connected to the fabric of Bill's improvisation. But I know
that I intend to go in and take that nugget of an idea and, on somebody
else's body, develop it. That's how I've been able to use the improvisations.

The improvisation is often transcribed by Janet Wong, my rehearsal
director. Thank God for her mind! And for her being able to sit with a vid-
eotape and fast forward and rewind. Once we decide on the improvisation
I want to work from, she will go home and learn it. She actually knows it
better than I do and can teach it to me and to the company. That's one way
of getting material.

It's also wonderful to build movement from the mind, asking myself,
"What if I did this, this, and this?" And then trial and error, trial and error;
make a little bit and master it, make a little bit more and master it. That's
also exciting. More difficult, more frustrating. And sometimes I just feel
it's not flowing, that it's coming too much out of the mind. It's got to be
something like breathing to be really good.

Another level of excitement is when this material is introduced into the
crucible that is the company: all those personalities and their various takes
on it, mistakes they make that shed light on what it could be. Suddenly
now there is a language that we all share and they, all thinking individuals,
begin to act on that language and take it to another level of interest. This is
how work is made. The proposition I had in the beginning might have
been completely overwhelmed by the rich permutations that they redeliver
to me after having learned what I made initially.

D-Man in the Waters by Bill T. Jones (photo Lois Greenfield)

Last Supper at Uncle Tom's Cabin by Bill T. Jones (photo Jeff Day)

Each of my recent works had its own source. *Verbum* started with a desire to dialogue with Beethoven's music and to bring to this dialogue the current information I was getting from my dancing. The music was in place before there was any movement. From there, I'm not sure whether I was drawn by the music itself or by the desire to ask questions of the music. *World Without/In* started with asking why don't I take difficult, modernist music and introduce it to the formal movement strategy of accumulations? And reaccumulations. And partnering and duets and trios coming out of accumulation ideas. The idea was inherent in the György Kurtag music, though in making the dance I worked mostly in silence. *Black Suzanne* grew out of a desire to have a work that was exuberant and strong and extremely athletic in the repertory. I found the music, Shostakovich's String Octet, opus 11, after I knew what I was looking for. And I began to conduct contact improvisation workshops with my company, trying to take them back to my beginnings and how I thought of contact work and partnering.

There is an almost manic period of ecstasy at the process of being in the studio—which is my favorite time—making the work, seeing an idea come together. Then comes that kind of strange, vertiginous drop when a work is made and you feel kind of empty, useless. You look at the dance and may find it good, or maybe not. Or it could be very good, but it may not have captured what you were feeling. Then there is a helplessness: "Is there always going to be this chasm between what I propose and what actually comes into the world?" So that's the cycle.

One has to balance one's ambition and one's doubts. Honesty, self-honesty especially, is difficult. Do I really have "it"? Now, what *is* "it"? Well, you look at your heroes and you see how much they did when they were your age and so on. Then the other part is, okay, well, what if you don't have "it"? Do you have the guts or the wherewithal to change? Stop doing this and do something else? I obviously don't.

At this point, knowing how vulnerable I am, I ask for the discipline of a practice. Meditation is a practice. And yoga is a practice. Can your art truly be one step in front of another on a journey, even though you don't know how long it will be? But you're committed to it and you're disciplined enough and you live enough in the moment to be able to understand the small epiphanies. I'm getting there. But I'm also the donkey behind the carrot—the carrot being the masterpiece that is right out there, that is going to say everything, that is going to vanquish all your doubts about what you've made or what anyone could say about it.

There have been times when I had a commission to make a piece and I realized I didn't like the parameters of the commission, or I didn't like my collaborator. But I had to do it. Usually, though, there are always at least two or three propositions simmering. I'm not proud to say that oftentimes the ones that get my attention are the ones that have been funded.

Let's face the economics of the dance world and how my company works. We set aside so many weeks of the year or the season and, if there is a commission, at the end of that period we're expected to have something to show. But the work did not necessarily begin at the beginning of this fourteen-week rehearsal period. I was already thinking about it maybe three years before, maybe in some other form. I hear some music and I will immediately begin to dream in pictures. Sometimes when I'm looking at another person's work, at a dance concert in particular, or a painting, I find that first I am intrigued but, before I know it, something in that work has opened a door to me, asking questions about my work, sometimes literally solving a problem I've run up against. Or I think, "Oh, the way he put together those two colors or the way this motif was shown from one medium to another, I wonder if in that piece of mine I introduced this décor element and that choreography I might get a similar effect." Now, in the meantime, I'm no longer looking at the work I originally was looking at. I'm thinking about my own work. That happens a lot. There usually are several disparate dances that have to be made some time in the future, and because I'm always afraid I'm going to be caught unprepared on the day when rehearsals start, I have these scenarios that I'm constantly building, which I suppose is thinking about the choreography.

We had a budget for the Lincoln Center Chamber Music Society performances and I knew I wanted three new pieces. The question from my office was, "How much time do you think it will take you to make a piece?" So I threw out a number: five weeks plus a week in the theater for tech and lighting. So I had to find a way with fourteen or fifteen weeks of rehearsal to make three works come out, knowing that in the premiere it might not be finished yet. Then, during the touring, the work continues to develop. It's scary as hell, but that's just the reality of the economics right now.

I'm a big reviser. Part of it comes out of not being sure. Also having in my mind a CD-ROM of possible ways it could have worked. When I've committed myself to one version, once it is completely convincing and satisfying to me and an audience, I will leave it. But most of the time some questions remain. You want to leave this work behind because probably you've got two or three more pieces that you should be doing. "But no," that work says, "no, no, no, you're not done with me yet." A certain sequence could have been richer. What about moving material from this other piece and putting it in there? And once it shifts, it's got to be attended to: transitions, proportions, endings. Once you've cut, you've got to smooth over. I've always been a kitchen sink kind of choreographer. When it's good, it's good. But when it's bad, it can collapse under its own weight.

Some revisions happen when new dancers come in. As much as I would like dancers to be interchangeable, they're not. So everything from costuming to partnering has to be reconsidered and sometimes tailored for that new person. I drive my dancers crazy. Sometimes before performances I say, "Tonight let's try doing this new arrangement in this place in the dance." They've got to be relaxed and willing to make a change. You can't throw inappropriate amounts of new material or instructions at them, but you can change little things. I try to position the dancers in such a way that they realize that the work is constantly growing, so that they can get interested. I do that by talking with them.

When a piece is about to be made I come in with the music and an idea and some movements and then I say to them, "You know, I'm feeling this right now. I'm asking myself this set of questions. Can you help me answer this?" Then they're invested. So later on, I can say, "You know, we worked through this, but I never felt that it was solved. Can we try this?" Now, sometimes they're angry and sore and tired and they're not so generous. Other times they'll say, "Well, yeah." Some of them say that's why they work with a living choreographer. Because they're part of the process. It's happening now.

When Arnie died I did not have to keep the company going. He even said so to me. He knew how flaky I am and that I'm not a great ensemble dancer. But I'm a people person. And I decided to keep the company. Therefore I built this enterprise and I continue to build it. And built into it is a sort of collaborative spirit. I call the ultimate shots—what the music is, the shape of the work, and what really goes into it—but I leave it wide open for people to give their best to it. I also need to feel connected to a larger world of creation through collaborators, musicians, and other artists. Consider a person who is a great artist in another medium: You're curious to be intimate with that person, spend time with them, and try to fashion something together. Through that contact I learn and I'm encouraged. Rejuvenated. That's important.

When I worked with Arnie we didn't even know we were collaborating, our lives and work were so intertwined. As for other collaborations, some of them were like hot and fast romances that were wonderful, wonderful, and then they just sort of fizzled. A one-shot deal. Some of them were slow getting started but I realized, if I looked around after some years, that I was still working with the same person. Take our lighting designer, Robert Wierzel. At first I didn't know if I could work with this guy. His tastes and his take on modern art and all didn't seem to be coming from the same place of urgency that Arnie and I were coming from. And now here it is twenty years later and he's one of my closest collaborators. I wouldn't even consider doing a piece without him. We really care for each other and I respect him. He's very good.

It also has happened that through fortune or circumstance, suddenly there was an opportunity to work with somebody who had been a big hero to me, a glowing icon in the distance. And it turned out to be a hellish and ultimately unsatisfying experience. So you almost wish you never had gotten so close to an icon. You don't want to have the allure taken away. Plus, in collaboration, rule one is you're dealing with a human being. Not with your press, not with some projection generated by the media. You're dealing with a real personality. I need to work with passion, with urgency. Sometimes I bore even myself with my need for urgency. Some other people just aren't that way. This is just another job for them. From my perspective, you want first of all for them to share their questions with you, what they find urgent or beautiful. Not all are willing to do it. Or you want them to be interested in your questions. And sometimes they're not. They have a persona or they have something that they do, that works for them. And they thought you were going to come in and be part of it. Sometimes we just can't accommodate.

We all know that this kind of art is not in the mainstream. How many people on a Friday night say, "Oh, what shall I do: read, go to a museum, go to a movie, go to a modern dance concert? Modern dance? Not interested." And that's back to this question of doubt, not only about me but about the form itself.

Arnie and I used to feel if you want to be in the avant-garde, really be a provocateur, you take your ideas from the preserved domain and carry them into the mainstream. That's what we thought was our strategy. That's how we justified our trendiness and our interest in pop art and fashion and so on. Now, as I get older, I like the idea of a preserved domain. I like an audience of people whom I don't have to dazzle in the way that Hollywood dazzles or even a ballet company dazzles. They're there with me because they understand the questions.

How could one not understand the connection between the emotional and the physical? How could one not understand what makes us social animals, that we actually all partake constantly in a social ritual that is built around the body? Some may not understand this. We, as dancers, are the scientists of this realm.

Ithaca, New York
March 25, 2002

10
Ann Carlson (b. 1954)

Growing up in the Chicago suburb of Park Ridge, Illinois, Ann Carlson took classes in ballet and modern dance. She majored in dance at the University of Utah, where she studied with John Wilson, who taught Margaret H'Doubler's anatomical and exploratory method of dance, and with Joanne Woodbury and Shirley Ririe. By following John Wilson to the University of Arizona at Tucson, she became the first graduate student in the new dance program he was developing. From graduate school she made her way to New York, where she evolved a choreographic style that is based on her predilection for what she calls "unadorned gesture." Despite her strong technical training, she has found her life's work in the exploration of movements arising from ordinary life. Her work presents imagery that seems nature-based but has cultural commentary embedded within it.

Carlson's work combines visual settings and projections, movement, and sounds that arise from her vocal investigations. One main focus has been her solo work, including the *Animal Series* in which she has performed variously with goats, dogs, a goldfish, and a kitten. These pieces have at times embodied movement based on her study of animal behavior, including that of a gorilla and a whale. In her *Real People* series she has worked with groups of lawyers, schoolteachers, fly-fishers, nuns, and horse wranglers, among others, developing dances out of the movements they do in their everyday lives. The "real people" themselves perform the pieces they helped create. Carlson has also made large-scale, site-specific performance installations, which have been done on a dairy farm, on a frozen pond, and within and alongside a train moving through Montana. These threads of her work have continued in parallel.

Ann Carlson has been awarded a Foundation for Contemporary Performance Fellowship, the Cal Arts/Alpert Award, and a three-year choreographic fellowship as well as seven consecutive years of fellowships from the National Endowment for the Arts. Carlson has also received the National Choreographer's Award, a New York Dance and Performance (Bessie) Award, the Met-Life Young Talent Award, a John Simon Guggenheim Fellowship, and a New York Foundation for the Arts Fellowship.

* * *

Ann Carlson in *visit woman move story cat cat cat* (photo Lois Greenfield)

Ann Carlson

I was born the second of three kids in Park Ridge, Illinois, a middle-class suburb of Chicago. My dad worked as the principal of a public middle school. My mom worked as well. At the age of six or seven I started studying ballet very seriously and continued until I was about thirteen or fourteen. I latched onto it; I loved its other-worldliness.

While I was studying ballet, I was secretively making up dances in the basement. From early on, part of my dance training was our being given stories and then dancing/acting them out. In the ballet class we did barre, then center, then a combination, and then there was a time set aside when we'd dance the stories of the ballets. The teacher would put a little music on and each child would get a turn being one of the characters. I have a strong memory of really enjoying that. And that informs what I do today. The roots of what I'm doing at age forty-eight can be traced to the things I felt passionate about at age eight. I guess there's also a downside to that. Does the path get so entrenched that you don't see out of it?

Somewhere along my preteen years, when I was about ten or eleven, I happened on a dance teacher who also did a lot of work in modern dance, which I tended to look down on. Nonetheless I took modern, too. My teacher asked me to come to a class taught by a gentleman who was going to be in town. She said it was going to be a modern dance master class. "Cut out your tights and roll them up." I remember rolling my eyes, thinking I wouldn't come. I said I was busy. She called me back and said, "You really need to come. You don't know this man, but it's important." The gentleman turned out to be Charles Weidman, one of the great modern dance pioneers. I have photos from it and remember it clearly. It was kind of an improvisation class using open structures and inventing movements inside of these structures. It turned out I really liked it.

Another event that was aesthetically pivotal for me was seeing a Murray Louis lecture demonstration when I was twelve. I remember his dancers being all barefooted in the downtown Chicago Museum of Contemporary Art. He talked about breaking down movement in space, time, and energy, and about all conscious movement being dance. He directed us in the audience to scratch our heads and then had us vary the timing—a very simple abstraction of a functional action. I remember thinking how profound that was. He said, "You can go home tonight and you can do a dance based on any kind of chore you have." Washing the dishes was my chore. I remember going home and breaking down the action and thinking, "I can make a dance out of this now. I don't have to take it into the studio; I'm making a dance right here." It was very powerful.

About the same time I had an experience at Ravinia, an outdoor festival space in the Evanston area where the New York City Ballet came in the summertime. A friend of mine and I went to see them and were sitting close to the stage. They were doing Balanchine's *Who Cares?* to Gershwin music. Something went wrong and the conductor went tap, tap, tap, and everything stopped. I remember an adrenalin rush through my body. When the dancers stopped, they dropped out of the imaginary world and suddenly their feet looked like duck's feet and their tutus flipped forward as they stood there. I had a strong visceral reaction to it: I suddenly saw ballet as a form. I realized I had been making a decision to study this form thinking the standards of ballet were the only way.

I felt an excitement at seeing that immediate break from the dancers' *doing* something to their *being* the *people* doing that something. It excited me visually, kinesthetically, and aesthetically. They stood there and stared at the conductor for a minute, then ran upstage, got into place, and started again. At the time, I didn't include that moment of their dropping out as part of my concept of dance. It looked so separate. That separation is what eventually really interested me and still does.

The other odd layer to this event was that my friend, who had been looking at her program, missed it all. It happened very fast. I had to wonder, "Did it happen at all?" I trust my memory that it did. But the person I was with didn't see it, so there's that wonderful bit of doubt, did I make it up? That story became the opening in my work *Grass/Bird/Rodeo* about authenticity of memory and what is real.

I studied modern dance more and more in high school and then went to undergraduate school in Utah. My parents encouraged me to go far away to college. They thought I should have an experience that was different from the suburbs. I remember feeling the suburbs were not representative of the way the world was. I felt boxed in there, although I got an incredible education. But there was only one black person who went to my school and I remember thinking, "This isn't right." Not that there were many black people in Utah either.

Initially, I asked the dance faculty if I could double major as a ballet and modern dancer and they looked me over and said no. Even though I certainly struggled with body image, it hadn't occurred to me that they would bar me from studying ballet. That was the beginning of my thinking, "Oh, you mean I'm supposed to be the way everyone else is? Why?" That moment gave me pause, but I just went into the modern department, which was amazing then. Bill Evans, who's very well known in the West, was there. Kathleen McClintock, who has since been at Mills College for years, was there. The Utah Repertory Dance Theater fed the department. Joanne Woodbury and Shirley Ririe were there. John Wilson had a double Ph.D. in dance and theater and taught Margaret H'Doubler's work. He brought her there a number of times so that I had the experience of studying with her. And then there was a constant flow of people from New York. I remember Lar Lubovich coming in and a number of Martha Graham people.

It was almost a conservatory experience. You could be exempted from all your liberal arts studies. You took a standardized test and if you had a basic liberal arts education, really high school level, you didn't have to take any courses other than dance. Looking back I wish I hadn't done that, but I was a teenager and all I wanted to do was take technique and dance. My body was ready to do that, so that's what I did, although I would always add in a course—embryology or various other subjects that I took pass/fail just because I was interested in them. In fact, I remember a lot about those subsidiary courses.

Then I followed John Wilson to the University of Arizona at Tucson, where he went to start a graduate program in dance. I ended up being the first grad student in a program that wasn't established yet, which was a difficult situation. I did a lot of work on neurological topics, like how the brain learns movement, and ended up with a master's degree in science. I worked with autistic children as part of my thesis. I also made a lot of work at the time and started to explore the use of the voice. "Issues in Contemporary Art" was a pivotal course for me. I didn't know much about the other arts at that point, even though I liked experimental work and site work. I discovered people who were working in the visual arts and using the body as canvas and surface—which felt very different from what I had been taught about the body as an instrument through which energy would pass and shape would be made. I learned about the early performance artists: Chris Burden, Vito Acconci, Eleanor Antin, and all those people who came out of visual arts but were doing performance, time-based work. I was very excited about what they were doing. It expanded the range of what was possible.

In grad school I did a rather obsessive repetition series. I repeated actions for as long as the audience could stand it. I thought of the movements as symbolic actions. I cut a watermelon for half an hour. I stood and rubbed my arm for a really long time. I was pushing up against authority a little bit, trying to break out of some set of assumptions. My performance was booed. I got in trouble; they weren't going to pass me. The repetition series was a direct result of trying to work in a more visual context. In my mind it was successful, but it was a terrible disaster to look at.

For one part of my graduate thesis show, I did a high-end technical piece while the performance area was being cleaned. I wanted to set up a situation where the viewers were forced to see whether they were going to watch the janitor or watch the dancer. My bet was that they were going to watch the janitor. People thought that was "throwing dance in the trash can." That was in the review. I just thought it was an interesting experiment.

I've always liked the look of unadorned gesture that is unrehearsed and unpracticed, like naïve painting. I remember the first time I went to the American Dance Festival after I finished grad school. It was in 1982 or '83. There I was, surrounded by high-technique, purposeful, exacting movement. I was also getting a lot of support at the time for my technical ability. But I saw Ze'eva Cohen's daughter, who was at most twelve years old and moved with incredible abandon, and I thought, "I must make a piece with her. Is there a way to sequence and frame and make that sort of abandon visible and full? Is it possible to codify it and structure it? Have it be repeated?" This was the start of the series that I later euphemistically called the *Real People* series. I find myself drawn to this type of seemingly not conscious movement. I had the girl put herself in a plastic bag at the end. I asked Ze'eva if it was okay. Ze'eva's daughter loved doing it because it went against a rule. I knew she wasn't going to suffocate. But there was a sort of horrification that passed through the audience. I don't want to pathologize or psychoanalyze, but what was I trying to smother?

I have worked more with people who aren't trained dancers than with those who are trained. Some people seem to think my defining myself as a choreographer and yet not working with dancers makes a political point and they resent the choice I've made. Twice people have confronted me on the street, letting me know they interpret my choice as a negative attitude toward dancers, which I don't consciously feel. I may turn my back on a traditional way of working, but I don't put down anybody else for working that way. Anyway, I do sometimes work with trained dancers, but I find most of the time I'm stripping them down, saying, "Drop it. Let go." I think that there was an area of my own training that was very painful on some level that pertained to becoming a "dancer."

When I came to New York City after grad school and ADF I auditioned for Meredith Monk. That was her retrospective year. I had never been to New York and, just like in the classic story, I came with only five hundred dollars in my back pocket. Working with Meredith was astounding to me. I thought, "Here's someone actually doing what I was merely aiming to do." And she had been doing it for a while. I soaked that up like a sponge. We did *Quarry* and *Book of Days* at Carnegie Hall. I was terrified of her at the time, but I volunteered for a vocal solo. When Meredith asked those of us in the big chorus, "Does anyone want to try this?" I raised my hand, and she said, "No, no you couldn't do it." Then I raised my hand again. So she let me try.

I had never sung publicly before, and my first public singing was at Carnegie Hall. That was funny to me, so I remember going back to my folks and saying that I had a solo at Carnegie Hall. They responded, "Wow, Ann." I said, "Do you want to hear it?" It was a repeated, rhythmic sound I made in my throat. That was my solo. My parents said, "I wouldn't go across the street to hear that." I said, "Well, that's what I'm doing in Carnegie Hall; it's part of a really amazing work." I credit Meredith with my interest in using the voice. I perceived her vocal music as her choreographing her voice.

I auditioned for Meredith again, and she took me into her office and said, "You must go make your own work. Stop doing my work." I sat on the curb and did a big boo hoo. I felt like I had gotten kicked out of the nest. I wasn't a young person; I was twenty-eight by that time. I'm so grateful for it now. I was already making some work, and she just said, "No. Go."

I had been taking Jocelyn Lorenz's ballet classes the whole time I had been in New York and enjoying them. But suddenly one day I couldn't go. I took myself there and I couldn't go up the stairs. I turned around and left. At the time I was very sad about it because class was almost like church. It felt like a deeply familiar ritual: It was community based; it was time to myself. But it had stopped being that, evidently, and had become somehow harmful. I hadn't intended to stop studying technique. I thought it was the way, even if you were going to experiment. In the Midwest, where I grew up, there's a rule structure that may never get expressed, but you live by it. I'm not so sure I didn't apply that to my own process: Of course, you take class every day.

Now what was I to do? I panicked. I had to find another way. I went into the studio and asked myself a crucial question: "What do you want to do?" That seemed completely radical to me. And blasphemous. But I found myself saying, "Okay, so here you are, you're almost thirty, and if this is what you are going to do, you need to make sure you enjoy actually doing the work. Not talking about it, not having the identity, not thinking about it. It has to be something that you like to do whether there's an audience there or not." Looking back on it, that was an important question. However I came to that question, I'm grateful I did.

I guess it didn't occur to me at that moment to make dances for other people, probably primarily for economic reasons. I had very limited resources. Moreover, I was interested in the solo form. I knew I could get myself in a studio, so I did. Plus not being able to go to technique anymore flew in the face of the whole tradition of "Here, I'm the choreographer, I'm going to show you. Do it like me." That whole paradigm didn't work anymore.

The trick in solo work is that you're limited to your own body. But I didn't feel at all limited at the time. I had so much fun. It was deeply fun. And that initial question was the literal crafting device for the movement: Do you want to do this? Not really. Then throw it out. It sounds self-indulgent, but saying it's self-indulgent is already from that other perspective—which is part of my training and will always be part of me. Of course you don't train for twenty-three years and then have the external eye and ear and judge not be there. But I just took over my own practice, and it was high time.

While it felt radical, it was an important realization for me that I could be guided by what I *wanted* to do. That became true with all of the animal pieces. Even in the one piece in that series that I'm not in, *Duck, Baby*, I followed that line with the dancers: "Does this hurt? Is this fun to do next?" Eventually that got to be a bit of a drag. There's a part of me that's a traditional choreographer that's thinking, "This gets time-consuming. It's easier to do this yourself than with others." Nevertheless, it has become a well-worn method that I use in making work. I ask people what they're interested in. Now that the *Real People* work, which began with having nondancers generate their own movements, has crossed over into working with dancers, they often don't know what to do with it. They prefer that I ask them fewer questions and get on with it. But I'm making the work out of their information and I need their input in the process.

Recently, I was working with a group of students for about ten days and had been encouraging them in their own agency as young dancers. I questioned them, "Are you ever asked by a choreographer to do anything that you find offensive? Do you stand up for that? Or do you concede that, no, this is such a good learning context, I'm going to override my personal beliefs?" So then when I said, "I want to have fat suits made for you all," trying to prick at a lot of issues and thinking it was a good metaphor for American consumerism, they said, "Absolutely not; we're not going to wear fat suits." One girl got teary-eyed about it, "I just will not." I had been talking to them about using their own agency, but now it came back to bite me. I had to let go of that plan. Then I realized I should just make a fat suit for myself.

In the late eighties, I got interested in a story that I had heard about goats that faint when they are afraid. During World War II, where tanks were coming into France, all the nearby goats fell over. The farmer said to the soldier, "You've killed my goats. I need to be repaid." So he was paid and the tanks went on their way and soon the goats all stood up again. The farmer was able to do that repeatedly. I thought what an interesting metaphor it was. One of my repetition series in grad school had been about falling, and I was still interested in that action and how much of it I could tolerate physically. I started playing with that story and also playing with falls—à la Doris Humphrey. The Maine Festival had also just invited me to make a piece. "Could you make something out-of-doors?" And I said, "Do you have any goats?"

I was interested to see how the goats would respond to movement. I made *Scared Goats Faint,* based on falling and running and falling and running. The dance ended up being done outside in a pen with goats. I had such a great time with the goats in Maine and an amazing time with the farmer. I asked, "Do your goats mind this, do your goats mind that?" I was treating the goats like pets. She made it clear to me that that wasn't her relationship with the goats. Her relationship was much more callous. Not mean at all and not cruel. Merely more distant, more utilitarian. It seemed so obvious on some level, but if you don't grow up agriculturally it's not at all obvious. In an urban or suburban context, you have a very different relationship with the natural world.

Not long afterward, I happened upon the *National Geographic* issue about Koko the gorilla, which I found extremely beautiful. I also had seen Simone Forti at the American Dance Festival do animal imitations in the context of the pieces that she was making. At that time I was giving myself from ten o'clock to twelve o'clock every morning to do anything I wanted and was going to the zoo a lot. It was a substitution for not going to technique class. I was observing gorillas, especially the weight of their gestures. How do I get my hands to feel the weight and both the articulation and inarticulation of that gorilla hand? I was trying to induce almost a trance or self-hypnosis in myself, trying to recover an ancestral memory of what it felt like to have those hands. It's a little far-fetched, but that was the process I was working with.

I've always been interested in sign language; I had studied it in undergrad school and was especially blown away by the idea of someone's teaching an animal to talk. There's been a lot written about the way Koko broke down language and used sign language in descriptions. She called a ring a "finger bracelet" and called an earthquake something like a "bad dark earth bite." I got the title of the piece by imagining what Koko would call it if she saw it. *Visit woman move story cat cat cat* is my interpretation of her syntax. I started reading about animal communication, including the book *Kinship with All Life* by J. Allen Boone. At the same time I was shaking up the whole concept of man's place among living creatures. The chain of animals is not a ladder, and it's not a pyramid. It's much more a circle. I was shifting my own worldly paradigm.

While I was caught up in watching live gorillas and thinking about Koko, I was listening over and over to one of Beethoven's string quartets, which I ended up using as the music for the piece. Then I started painting my whole body dark black-brown and jumping around in the apartment. From watching gorillas every day, I think there was a body-level acceptance going on. I was really interested in evolution. I went to the Museum of Natural History and started looking at skeletons. On some level my body knew about the transitional being between the apes and humans; in some way I felt I had been through it and had a connection to the collective unconscious via a genetic, neurological pathway. I consciously brought these elements together: the music, the interest in that transitional creature, the story of Koko's caretaker's giving her a pet cat, and Koko's mourning of the cat's death.

During this period I also was doing "Effort Shape" work with Irmgard Bartenieff's protégé Mieke van Hoek. I was new to that body-level work and was curious about different body disciplines that were outside of the traditional training. I kept telling her that I felt a kind of black, furry ball in my solar plexus and didn't understand it. She had a practical response, "Maybe you should go get x-rayed," but she also said, "Stay with that feeling." She guided me and directed me toward trusting those imagistic body-level experiences. About three quarters of the way into the process of making the dance about Koko, I made the cat connection, "Oh, that's the ball of fur." It was such an obvious allegorical grief story.

At the same time, around 1986, Mark Russell had started the Performance Space 122 Field Trips for which he gathered a group of people together to tour. We went to Bennington College, where I was given a space to work in. It was a huge gift. I spent a lot of time with a kitten and a lot of time all by myself. I made a commitment that I would be in the space for eight hours a day. It didn't feel grueling. The piece uses music visualization, although it was also the first time I played with a structure of what I call "fence post choreography," where I was working primarily with qualities of movement based on what someone from a theatrical background might call "character." The piece wasn't choreographed step by step, but with a generalized plan: I know I'm going to cross here and then

I'm going to do this type of movement. Because it was a solo, I had an enormous amount of play, literally and figuratively, with the work.

In this piece I spend some time totally still and some time moving through the space, some time holding a live kitten, and some time on a jungle gym that I had built for the dance. Working on the jungle gym and getting really comfortable with it ended up taking most of my eight hours each day for almost a year of working. It also took me a long time to decide to do the piece naked. I initially did it with underpants on. The topless part wasn't an issue. But because the Field Trips had started to tour, I performed it more and more in many different places. People would come up to me and say, "The underpants just aren't right. You need to get rid of them." About a year and a half, maybe two years into the piece, I did get rid of the underpants. It was a big deal, though I was comfortable enough with it by that time.

I have so many stories about touring with that piece and producers being subpoenaed because of different city council ordinances that a woman can't be naked with an animal on the stage, back from the time of traveling circuses. "Would I please just put an undershirt on?" I was so amazed. Call it naïveté, but when I was making the work, I never gave any of that any consideration. None. And yet it became such a big deal, at least outside New York. Producers would come to me and say, "You can't do it naked. We bought you this teddy." A negligée. So I said, "That's going to sexualize the piece. That's going to be really weird for people. Trust me, it's not weird for them to see it naked." That's why I squat there in profile for a good four minutes, so people can take it in and relax.

I still do the piece, though I haven't done it publicly since 1997. It would be an interesting piece to continue to perform as I'm aging, but I don't know if I have the guts. I think it would be interesting because it pushes at the boundaries of the wonderful unselfconsciousness that animals have and that I was trying to get underneath and behind and into. The animal in oneself. Could I invite the audience to look at me the way they look at an animal? To look differently, to perceive differently. Really it was an invitation for myself. To be moving, dancing, celebrating; it was celebratory inside that story of grief.

My thinking gets completely exposed in *visit woman move story cat cat cat*. When my work is most successful, the conceptual framework and the movement are evenly weighted. The thinking strategy and the movement research all pour into the same structure. When it works right, it allows you to experience the thinking and the feeling as part of the work. I don't always hit that. *Visit woman move story cat cat cat* hit it, I think.

My *Animal Series* was initially a suite of five dances that are performed on the concert stage. Since that time, I have done outdoors animal pieces performed on site. Animals had a specific role in my family. Our attention and expression and emotion for each other filtered through the animals. That was the currency of discourse as I was growing up. If you wanted to get to my dad, you talked about the dog. It was really that clear. Even though my dad was a lovely, gentle man, he had a hard time expressing emotion. But a kid knows your currency. I interpreted information about the dog as a kind of information about myself. I loved the dogs, but I also resented them. Get the dogs out of the way, let's have a direct conversation.

Now I look at the *Animal Series* and see the source layer that runs through it. The personal myth inherent in the series had so much to do with my upbringing. Not unlike the family dog, I, too, went through a kind of domestication in my dance training; I've both valued it and bridled at it. And the mixture of love and resentment I've felt toward animals I've also felt toward dancers. I've found, as I look back, that this combination of feelings has propelled a lot of my curiosity.

We don't have animals in my current family, other than hamsters and fish and the like. But I still do pieces with animals. I love the idea of gently including an animal onstage without manipulating it. Of course, it's a manipulation because it's an artificial environment, but I like setting up that potential. I've tried to stop many times but it just keeps coming up. Although I don't think the work is there to be therapeutic, I do think there is a layer of something I long to have completed or filled up or answered, even if it's never articulated.

While making the *Real People* work, which I've been doing over a span of more than fifteen years, I often shadow people to see what their day is like, what their life is like, what their profession is like. I've had amazing experiences being a fly on the wall in all of these circumstances. I've made pieces with lawyers, nuns, basketball players, fly-fishers, fiddlers, school-teachers, and a whole other assortment. I work with them in making the piece, and they are ultimately the performers. After following them around for a period, at some point I ask them to come together and start working gesturally. The lawyer piece, from 1986, started by my saying, "Can you just grab your arm like this?" and "I notice that you knock on things a lot. Can you knock on the floor?" I'll usually give them the reason immediately; as I sequence the movement I remind them of their day's context for that gesture.

Ann Carlson in *Grass* section of *Grass/Bird/Rodeo* (photo Ross Kolman)

Ann Carlson in *Bird* section of *Grass/Bird/Rodeo* (photo Ross Kolman)

I think of the *Real People* dances also as contemporary folk dances. Some of the people I made the dances with have repeated them without a performance context, just to do it. It's similar to my saying to myself, "Do you want to do this whether you're performing it or not?" They're saying yes to that question. A number of years after the group of lawyers had been performing the piece, one of them was getting married and I was invited to the wedding, as were the other lawyers in the group. The groom wanted to do the piece at his own wedding. So we went back in the kitchen and they rehearsed it and then went out and did it. They didn't really need me. That's where I thought, "This is like folk dance even though they were the only ones who could actually do it; not everyone could participate." It was mostly a lawyer community at the wedding, so there was a special layer of recognition. They laughed or responded and participated in a very different way than other audiences had. I made a piece for a board of directors out west. They, too, ended up performing it when they got together. That started to expand my sense of this activity that we know so well when it takes place on stage, opening it up to being less of a Westernized proscenium stage performance in a rarified space and making it be right in our lives.

These days I'm spending time with doctors who work at Children's Hospital in Boston, ultimately intending to make a work. I'm not sure what the form of the work will be. Right now I'm just absorbed in the research and really enjoying it. Although I've long had an interest in medicine and the way the body works, I find that the way doctors actually spend their days is foreign to me. But there's the problem that, even though these doctors have agreed to do this and—like everybody else— have an interest in looking at the metaphor of their daily life, it turns out that they have no time. So to do time-based performance work with them is a particular challenge. I'm realizing it's really not possible. I tried to make this piece before and it didn't get made then either. But the doctors are the only ones who can do those gestures in the way that they can do them; they're the ones who should perform it. This isn't about translating their movement onto other performers. Yet the piece won't get made if I don't find a different process for making it.

Dead was made right after the *Animal* pieces, in 1989, for the opening of the sculpture garden at the Walker Art Center. It used seventy-five people and a horse. I saw it as a ritual about passing from this life to the next. I'd had inklings about the piece for some time. Then my dad passed away and that got me started. I went on to work on a piece called *West*, a collaboration with Mary Ellen Strom for the Museum of Contemporary Art in Los

Angeles. I got support from the museum. They were so generous in helping us make this work. When I went to them and said, "I'll need a horse," they didn't bat an eyelash. They bought me a horse, which I kept in a backyard stable in California, where we had moved to work on this commission. It was an amazing time, a fight-or-flight experience just getting myself prepared. The horse seemed so big. I was training really hard, doing a lot of work on the ground around the horse, and playing with what I knew was a dangerous situation. Then, during an early performance, I took a bad fall and lost my memory for a day. The audience thought that my falling off was part of the dance. I loved that. Despite that concussion, I still went on to work with the horse since I wasn't finished with the piece.

The story of my fall ended up giving rise to the next work, the *Rodeo* section of *Grass/Bird/Rodeo*. In fact, all of *Grass/Bird/Rodeo* was a response to the experience of making other works. I find that happens more and more now. *Blanket*, in which I wore so much padding and became quite unrecognizable, was a lot about having performed naked for so many years. There's a nice quote, though I can't remember who said it, about how one's current work is repairing boundaries that were broken from the previous work. As I look back, I think that it's true and relates to my sense of the organism on every level lunging toward wholeness or completion. I think it's true in terms of work, in terms of life, and in terms of the body and all of the components that make up being human. There's a kind of paradox in which repairing one boundary becomes breaking the next one, becomes repairing, oops, broke that one, becomes repairing, oops, and so on. It gives you the next thing to do.

I deal with anxiety daily, if I'm really honest about it. I have to wade through enormous amounts of it now even to get into the studio because the pressures feel greater; it feels like there's more at stake. One pressure is financial. Also there's the question, "Is it okay to still do work?" It was easy as a younger artist to paint myself black and run around the apartment. That kind of freedom is harder to access now, I'm sorry to say. Of course, just three years ago I said, "I think I want to be part burlesque dancer and part bird," and went on to make new work based on that. So maybe the truth is that I still follow my impulses. I get propelled by certain images—"Oh geez, I've really got to have a wing," or, "I love this bird/burlesque thing." It's interesting that my inspiration is so often connected to animals. Now I'm starting to think, "Has it ever not been animal based?" That ball of black fur. I'm not being driven right now by anything that is compelling me to figure out what it is. I'm not energized by an idea or a body-level impulse right now. Of course, the initial source is never highly articulated at the time that it happens, so maybe there is something that I'm doing currently that I'll look back on at some later time and think, "See, that was the genesis of what I'm doing now."

I've been working in stillness for the last three years, with other dancers. I've been engaged in recreating history, restaging archival photos in the location where they were originally taken, in the tradition of *tableaux vivants*. The viewer sees the tableaux along a walking tour so that they become like dioramas. I've been asked to do that in a number of different cities. I arrange it so that the local people who have invited me are the ones who decide on the photos they want me to recreate. That's gotten me involved in the question of who's in our history and who's in our archives. More to the point, who's *not*. There are often no people of color; there are no women. Photos of women are in a separate file in a lot of the main archives in cities around the country.

I'm working on a new piece that's going to happen out in Montana. It's a collaboration with Mary Ellen Strom. It was her idea intially. The audience goes on a train and on the nearby rock faces there will be video projections. I'm restaging tableaux alongside the route of the train, so the passengers will see them out the window. We're also working with Crow Indians to make *Real People* pieces inside the train. I'm excited about that. It's very large scale, a new scale of the *Real People* pieces. We're thinking about it as a conceptual tourist attraction.

New York City
November 22, 2002

11
Mark Morris (b. 1956)

Mark Morris was born and raised in Seattle, where at age nine he began studying flamenco and then ballet with Verla Flowers. It was clear from the start that his dancing had a deep rhythmic sense. At age thirteen—the same year that he began making his own pieces—he took up Balkan folk dance and began to perform with the Koleda Folk Ensemble. This group became a center of community for him and a utopian locus of singing and dancing.

Morris came to New York in 1976. The first performance of his work with a group of dancer friends in 1980 initiated the Mark Morris Dance Group and gained him immediate acclaim. In 1988 the Mark Morris Dance Group began a three-year tenure as the official dance company of the Théâtre Royal de la Monnaie, the national opera house of Belgium. Having space and funding for dancers, singers, and instrumentalists allowed him to make large works such as *L'Allegro, il Penseroso ed il Moderato* to music by Haydn and *Dido and Aeneas* to music by Purcell. Not much later he began to collaborate with Mikhail Baryshnikov on the White Oak Dance Project, a small modern dance company under Baryshnikov's direction that has performed Morris's works.

Mark Morris is noted for his close study and intimate understanding of the music he chooses for his dances and for his use of live music in all his performances. He has choreographed to popular songs, contemporary classical pieces, and Indian raga, though he has more often used baroque and classical music because of his abiding appreciation for their clear structures. Like his musical tastes, his dances range widely. Examining love, he's shown its exaltation in *New Love Song Waltzes*, its twisted pain in *Jealousy*, and its sly animal mountings in *Dogtown*. Morris has been called a classicist because of his formal clarity, the heir to traditional modern dance because of his sweeping phrases, and an *enfant terrible* who loves to shock his audience.

Among his many honors are grants from the Lila Wallace-Reader's Digest Fund and the Mellon Foundation, a John Simon Guggenheim Fellowship, and a MacArthur "Genius" Award. He was the subject of a PBS one-hour special. His work has been commissioned by the San Francisco Ballet and the American Ballet Theatre. In 2001 the Mark Morris Dance Center opened in Brooklyn.

* * *

Mark Morris in *O Rangasayee* (photo Lois Greenfield)

Mark Morris

Verla Flowers was my teacher from age nine, and a genius. She died just last week. When I was her student I wanted to make up dances, and she let me. I was maybe thirteen when I first had a piece presented on the stage. She gave me rehearsal time and the dancers I wanted and didn't question me about any of it. That's what got me going as a choreographer. I'd seen dances, of course, but I wasn't consciously trying to emulate any of them. I didn't know enough to do that. Then, when I was at a dance camp at age fifteen, we showed our student choreography at the end of the summer. That's where I did the first dance that was good, called *Barstow*, to Harry Partch's music. It wasn't that I wanted to be a choreographer when I grew up. I made up dances and then I was a choreographer. In that order.

Making a dance is like building anything: First you do this, then you do this, and then it's done. It's a job. I don't start with a big theater idea. Instead, I might need a particular kind of dance for my repertory, or I want to work with music by some composer, or some dancer hasn't done anything for a while, or I have new people in the company. As soon as I get new people I try to do a new dance for them so they're not merely learning other people's roles.

The dances all get made sort of the same way. Before I do anything else, I choose the music. I listen to it and study it and analyze it to whatever extent is needed to get a dance going. Or if it's not working I drop it. I've started the *Two Part Inventions* of Bach maybe three times in the last fifteen years and it just hasn't happened yet. But it will. I've learned that even pro-crastination is valuable work, so it doesn't bother me anymore. Putting off stuff is another way of getting excited about it.

I start either with the section I have no idea about, which is the part that's driving me crazy, or with the section I've been thinking about all the time that will take only a couple of days to make. Starting to work on some section, I may have an idea that it is all on a diagonal, or it has no partner-ing, or it is done only by men. All that may still change, but that's how it begins. I do all the work in the studio with the dancers. In rehearsal I make some moves I think might work. Then I change it. And then it turns into the material for the dance. Or not. That's all right.

If I decide that one section is going to segue into another section in ways I didn't predict, I may have to reposition people. Then it's, "Oh shit, I need everybody over there. How do I get you there?" Change something earlier? Or reposition them between movements? Or change personnel? You change one thing and it changes someone's track through the whole piece. But since everybody knows all the material, that's not so difficult to work out.

I don't necessarily start at the beginning and work through to the end, so "finishing" doesn't mean making the end of the piece. The parts that still need to be completed could be somewhere in the third movement. Usually the last part is anxiety producing because the language has already been established and I'm not going to introduce new elements just for the sake of finishing it. I have to drop in the keystone in the language that exists. In Charles Rosen's genius book *The Classical Style*, there's a chapter on Haydn trying to finish his pieces. He had the same problem. Great! I have the same problem as Haydn? I like that.

Even after all the material has been set, there are usually stylistic refinements. Maybe a step that was in there has to be changed because of how the rest of it goes. Or this part is now too complicated and I'm going to simplify it a little bit. I might change skipping to walking. Or I take stuff out. I do that all the time. Even after it's been performed I occasionally make adjustments if I see that I've put somebody going the wrong way and it doesn't make logical sense. But mostly I leave things alone once the show opens. Releasing a dance to the public is a pleasure but, you know, I've already sort of lost interest in it by then.

People have written some pretty strange things about how I make dances to music. When I work with music, it's certainly not a translation, or then anybody who choreographed the same music would do the same dance. Once I find a piece of music, it's not automatic that the dance *looks* like the music *sounds*—because there's no such thing. That's a complete fallacy. If I'm going to do something that's a fugue, I bring in themes and subthemes and counterthemes, and then manipulate those in the way that the music does. Or if I'm doing something that's a theme and variations, then I have to have a theme that is simple enough and rich enough that it can be varied. But it has to already be interesting alone. Of course, you don't have to parallel the music; you can do whatever you want. Ignoring the music is also an option.

When I'm not listening to music to work on a dance, I'm listening to music because I like it. If you love your job, then the boundary is less distinct. I read scores for fun. I don't read scores just for homework. You don't have to be able to read music to make up dances; but if you're going to make up dances to music, you'd better know what's going on, especially if you're going to work with musicians and conductors and singers. It's pathetic otherwise.

In finding movement for a canon, it has to be interesting and it has to link back in counterpoint with itself. There have to be some high and low levels, or how can you subject it to any sort of visible transformation? You can't effectively invert a phrase of movement that is on one level. There are other musical devices you can use as well. If you want the resolution of some particular cadence to also be the downbeat of the next segment, you have to build that in. First, you can make a phrase that's seventeen beats long so that it leads one beat into what comes next. If the next movement phrase starts before the first one is done and if the beginning of the second phrase is choreographed to be the same as the end of the first, they join briefly in unison. That's Haydn, that's not me. So it's not a secret trick. I like canons, but I don't use them as much as people say I do. In dance, it's much easier to see time designs than to see space designs, like the geometry of floor pattern or depth in the space or variations of height. People think in terms of canons, so they think they're recognizing one even when what they're seeing isn't necessarily a canon. Forms of repetition and imitation in time, canon included, are in every bit of music. There are all sorts of voice leadings and fugal structures and imitations that aren't necessarily canonic at all.

I work only with live music in rehearsal and class. I rehearse with a piano to avoid working from a particular recording. Why should that one recorded interpretation determine the way it's done? If there will be a chorus and a big orchestra when we perform, I'll play the recording for the dancers so they can recognize what it will sound like. But in rehearsal we'll use a piano reduction score. I can say to the dancers, "We're starting from the development section of the first movement." Or I can say to the pianist, "We're starting when those two enter." It can go either direction. That way nobody's accompanying anybody else. We're doing the same thing at the same time. That's my goal if I'm doing an opera, if I'm working with a ballet company, or if I'm with my own company. I don't want part of it to run the other part of it. I want it all to completely and exactly coordinate.

A couple of years ago I was asked to do a piece for four men at American Ballet Theatre. It was to be for a television special and they wanted a piece around seven or eight minutes long choreographed specifically for them. I didn't want to use a pastiche of music; I wanted to use one piece of music that's through-composed. I chose the last movement of a Schumann piece I had known for probably thirty years. (I realized while I was working on it that I had long ago danced to that music in a work by Hannah Kahn.) That last movement of the Schumann is symphonic in scope, a giant piece of music for five players. It includes the fabulous small fugue at the end that develops the musical material originally presented in the first movement. I choreographed that section for ABT, then the gig was postponed for a year. I meanwhile realized I wanted to do the whole piece for my company, which became the dance *V.* So last summer, while I was starting to work with my company on movements one, two and three, I was at the same time rehearsing with the gentlemen from ABT on movement four.

I wanted the dance for my company to use as many people as I could. Because I have sixteen in my company, that meant fourteen people, so I'd still have someone who could cover from each sex in case somebody got hurt. I'm not going to cancel a piece for lack of a replacement. To take advantage of the repeat schemes in the music, I set it on two teams, the blues and the greens. The blue people start in one V and the green people start inverted in the space. And because there are seven in each team, and there are an even number of men and women altogether, one group has four men and three women and the other has four women and three men, which affects everything. Anything that's not a simple line of seven I still wanted to be symmetrical from the center. Seven people align well in a V. That's what made it turn out to be Vs. The title came much later.

In the slow movement there's a walking sequence I made up. For a long time they're just walking, stepping on the third beat, then on the sixth beat. It wasn't necessarily to the musical phrase; it was subdivided. I wanted a kind of lurching, halting walk. So I decided to make one group move on the upbeats and one on the downbeats, and then they switch occasionally. I worked for probably a couple of weeks with a lot of variations on that, both complicated and simple. And then I put the dancers down on all fours because I wanted them to look like they were crawling up a wall. And that was exactly right. I made up all the rhythms and almost everything in the piece, but once I put it down low, it became exactly appropriate to this sort of getting nowhere and the semifunereal music.

In making the piece for my company, the fourth movement was the last one I made; it's similar to what I had done for the ABT gentlemen. Some of the structure is almost identical for the four ABT men and for the fourteen people in my company, and a lot of the moves are the same. But of course it's entirely different because of who's in it. And by the time we get to the final fugue, my dancers have the first movement of the piece to refer to, whereas the ballet, which consists of only the fourth movement, doesn't. The final fugue returns to the initial movement material, which is an arm gesture: open, close. Although it's more complicated in the fugue, the blue group essentially does close, open, close, open, and the green group does the opposite: open, close, open, close. When they're side by side it has one look. But in the fugue each dancer in blue is facing someone in green, so it has a different effect, and looks like a series of quick embraces. Some critic said it was too "huggy," that Schumann isn't "huggy." I agree, Schumann is not huggy, and neither is my dance. That's not what they're doing. If you could remember back twenty-five minutes to the first material you would recognize that the two themes are now arranged to face opposite each other; coincidentally it becomes an embrace, which, by that point in the piece, means something. It isn't, "I need a hug."

When reviews bother me it's because the journalists are reviewing a dance that they wish had happened instead of the one that existed. From my side, "I'm sorry you didn't like it, but it wasn't a mistake; they're doing what I want them to. It's not that I just didn't have any more ideas; this is the one I decided on." Or they say, "I loved the piece except for the ending." "Well, guess what, I tried the ending you wanted and it was the stupidest thing in the world, so I did my ending because it's my dance, and sorry if you don't like it." There are also the people who read a complicated interpretation into any dance they've seen. "Well, hooray for you, you have a very active imagination. That's wonderful." Then some people assume that everything that one does is autobiographical. How ridiculous! That's a bizarre notion on the part of people who don't really understand art very much. It's like assuming that the character someone plays on TV is that person's real personality. Of course that's part of it, but, come on, use your brain.

Confidence and arrogance aren't the same thing. If you have confidence without doubt, then I think you're just an idiot. Then you live in fantasy land. I think about what I do. Of course it gives me the greatest feeling of satisfaction and gratification that people love our shows. And I'm very happy and satisfied when I make up a beautiful dance. I hope that I'm smart enough that if I don't like what I'm doing, I'll stop it. But I love it. I have a great time and the company's fabulous. So I'm working.

We work either five- or six-day weeks. On a rehearsal day we usually have class at 10:30 or 11:00 in the morning. I teach an hour-and-a-half class, then we rehearse for about an hour and forty-five minutes until an hour lunch break, and then we rehearse usually until 6:30 or 7:00 in the afternoon. That's another three or three and a half hours. Different people are in different rehearsals. And now with the new building I can rehearse more than one thing at a time, so some dancers are putting stuff together from video or reviewing material in one room while I'm working in another space, rehearsing something else.

I like to work on two new pieces at the same time. If I have a four-week or five-week rehearsal period, I don't want to work on the same piece for six hours a day because that way I wouldn't get anything done. When you're doing the same movement many times, it fucks you up physically.

It's also not interesting. The maximum I would work on a new dance in a day is about two to three hours. Sometimes I'll work on one dance and then after a break I'll work on another dance or another section of the same piece. If I work on something that has a bunch of lifts or jumps in it, we do it for a while, and then I stop because I don't want people to get hurt. Once I've got the idea sufficiently I don't need to keep seeing it, so I say, "Take a break and we'll come back and do something new." I don't know what that's going to be necessarily. I work fast and the dancers work fast. I can do twenty versions in an hour. It's not a problem at all. And remembering is not a problem because, while you might misremember something, there's always somebody who does remember.

I'm busy with all sorts of different things that I have to do every day. The company is off this week and I taught a workshop in which I met with the same group every day for a couple of hours. I taught a technique class and did one million other things: meetings and design consultations and computer stuff and studying music. Yesterday I took a Pilates class, I taught class, I had a meeting with one of the dancers, I went to the dermatologist, and then I went to *Parade* at the Met. And the day before I watched a showing by one of my dancers and I had a massage and I had an interview and I had a meeting with my management and, you know, it goes on like that.

I care about everything that comes out of our office. I proofread all of the mailings. I delete exclamation points, reduce the number of commas, correct spelling, and simplify grammar. I decide every color of every brochure that goes out. The T-shirts, the merchandise, the way we present ourselves—I decide all of that. Color swatches and typefaces are Federal Expressed to me. I work with people I trust, but everything is cleared with me because if I see something that has my name on it and it's horrible, that upsets me. If it's horrible and I chose it, that's all right. But I don't want somebody else's stuff with my credit. I design costumes for some of my pieces. Or we shop it out. I go to fittings. I'm very interested and concerned in all of it. I'd love to be able to delegate more than I do. But even when I delegate, I still proof it. If something doesn't work, we throw it away and start over.

Of course, being in this new building has made a difference. It's not that we couldn't work before. It's just that it was a big pain in the ass to work someplace that's a piece of shit. And the conditions under which people are willing to work are embarrassing and demoralizing. A good example is the studio where Paul Taylor worked for years. As far as I can tell, the floor is cement with maybe wood over it. It's right on Broadway and it's noisy

V by Mark Morris (photo Robbie Jack)

Sang Froid by Mark Morris (photo Marc Royce)

and un-kept-up. They haven't had a coat of paint in years. It looks like what it would turn into if teenage boys lived there. It's filthy dirty and it's ugly and uncomfortable and the ceiling's low and the floors are way too hard. When I used to rehearse there I encouraged my dancers to wear running shoes because it was dangerous to dance on that floor. Meanwhile, Mr. Taylor's dancers are jumping and doing all this stuff on their knees. I wouldn't ever make anybody jump in that room. I'm not talking about Mr. Taylor's choreography; I'm talking about the situation where his company rehearses. I think it's debased. And that's a successful and popular company. To me there's something seriously wrong with that. This isn't a vacation. We work very hard. Our new space makes it easier because the floors are great and it's comfortable and the windows open and it's where we live. The situation is much better and it has a feel of respect to it. So that's great. But making up a dance is still impossible and dancing all day is still really, really hard.

I don't know why people put up with bad work conditions. Money isn't the only reason, believe me. It's a question of desire and insisting on what you want. There are things that we've had to do just for financial reasons. People ask, "Oh, my God, how did you get that space?" And the answer is that we worked on it for years. And raised money. I've had a company for twenty-two years and it's not a hobby and it's not pretend. It's an actual job that adults have. Unfortunately, even a lot of adults who are dancers don't believe that. And so of course you're always going to be in the back drawer of attention in the art world. Dance is always a marginal form. That doesn't mean it has to have terribly low standards. Selling yourself short really bothers me.

There was a funny article in the San Francisco paper yesterday talking about the problem of ballet companies performing with live music. And then there was a quote from me: "Mr. Morris' company only performs to live music and here's why: because he insists on it." I thought that was funny. It's not that easy. It's a lot of work and it's expensive. It wouldn't be bad if it were a matter of, "Oh, let there be live music!" In that case why wouldn't everybody just insist on it and then it would happen? It's not that simple. I have to figure: I won't do this unless I have an orchestra, but we can't afford a big orchestra. Okay, I'll do chamber music. Or okay, fine, I'll have a pianist. I won't have a synthesizer but I'll have a piano.

You can always put on a show at P.S. 122 with no money and have a friend sing or play the guitar or clap. A friend of yours who goes to Juilliard who loves to perform an incredibly difficult piece of Liszt could play while you dance. No problem. You can do that. You don't have to use taped music. Of course if the piece is written for tape or that's the effect that you want for that show, or it's a historical recording or a piece by Morton Subotnick or the like, then you have to have recorded music. Of course, then they have shitty speakers, but that's another story.

My management says that I'm not good at collaborating with people but that's not entirely true. It is just that I often have a strong idea about what I want, which limits what can happen with a collaborator. Otherwise you could work the independent way Merce Cunningham does, which is a beautiful way of working that produces something wonderful. But I don't want to say, "Look, you play some music, you design some sets, and we'll all show up together and my company will dance." I'm not interested in that method for myself.

I don't work with composers very often partly because it's so arduous and you never know what you're going to get. So I'm reticent about commissioning new music. There's so much fabulous music already. In the design elements, I usually know what I want and somebody realizes it for me. I say to my lighting designer, "It's too dark there. I can't see them." But it's not always about me getting my way. I can also rely on my designers to come up with suggestions. I may have no idea what I want, and the set designer or costume designer listens to the music and we talk about it. I work with the same people a lot because I trust them and they're very good.

I made up some dances in Seattle, some in Brussels, and some in New York, and I suppose they're different partially for that reason. I would hope the work keeps changing over the years. Otherwise, you've make up the same dance over and over for your whole life. I've seen that done way too many times. I think that if you're an artist who is halfway decent at what you do, you essentialize and simplify and make more direct. You waste fewer gestures and you try to make it exactly itself, exactly pure. I think my work is getting clearer. For some people that means dryer or less purple than it used to be. That's fine with me.

I like to have old dances in the repertory just because they're different from the new dances. And people like to watch them. If I'm sick of a dance and everybody loves it, we'll still do it, though I won't have that much interest in it and would prefer to drop it. *Gloria,* which was around for way too long, will be fine to bring back in a few years; but I don't want to see it now. We rotate repertory. We did many, many performances of the Chopin piece *Sang Froid* a couple of years ago. It's a beautiful dance and it kept getting better. But enough already. We'll drop it for now and come back to it.

Going into the studio and working with the dancers is my favorite thing. Of course, the dancers change over the years but they're not just replacing each other. They all have different lives and different experiences and different histories. In some way my dancers now are technically superior to those of fifteen years ago—but that's not quite the point. The dances have changed and the dancers have changed. Sometimes an old dance done by new people might look really weird. Or somebody from fifteen years ago may not work well doing the newest dance I made up. My work is harder than it seems. But all the material in my dances can be done by anybody in the company—not because I aim to the lowest common denominator but because they're all at a high level. If I do something that's hard for certain dancers to do, they'll learn how to do it by the time they have to perform it.

My dancers have to dance great. That's the main thing I care about. But we also spend a lot of time together, so we have to get along. They have to be smart, because I don't like to spend a lot of time with real idiots. Everybody is very good for different reasons. I'm not best friends with every one of them, but at least they can read books and have a conversation and drive a car and get from here to there and live in the world and remember a lot of stuff and work really hard and not get injured much.

I don't work with other dancers often. I don't sell any dances that were made on my company to anybody else, although we do lend work cheaply to universities. A particular college class might learn a piece or an excerpt of my work. We send somebody in to work with them and they perform it; and that's fine. But I don't sell work to other modern dance companies at all, ever. I sell only my ballets.

When I work with an outside ballet company now, I rent them a dance that already exists and then I do the casting. I send someone else to teach it. I see it and then decide whether I want to make up a new dance for them. But I've had it happen several times where I go in and make up a new dance, which is a lot of work, and I come back for a show and it doesn't look like my dance anymore. It looks like a bad Balanchine piece or a bad Gerald Arpino piece—or a good Gerald Arpino piece. Not my piece at all it. If I come back and it looks like a Bournonville piece, I'm happy. But I don't want it Balanchinized, even though I could say with no qualms that the two best choreographers of the twentieth century are Merce Cunningham and George Balanchine. But I work hard to get a particular kind of action and dynamic and tone to the piece. And if you don't have that, you don't have the dance.

I've done five or six pieces for the San Francisco Ballet. I go back because they're great and they maintain my work. They work with an orchestra that is quite good. So I made a piece for them using music for a big orchestra. I also was there for the orchestra rehearsals. But I'm not going to risk making up a dance for City Ballet and have that awful orchestra play something that is just horrific. Why bother with that? It's not worth it. If you have a pretty dance that's being driven by a ghastly piece of music or one that's played horribly—I'm sorry, life's too short for that. Life's too short to listen to shitty orchestras. You may quote me on that.

Brooklyn, New York
March 29, 2002

12

John Jasperse (b. 1963)

John Jasperse grew up in Rockville, Maryland, a suburb of Washington, D.C., and began taking dance classes during high school. Upon graduating from Sarah Lawrence College in 1985, where he studied liberal arts and dance, he immediately began making group work. Between 1987 and 1993 he worked with Jennifer Monson, who encouraged him to explore bold movements that felt uncharacteristic for his tall, thin body type. He also performed with Anne Teresa de Keersmaeker's company, Rosas, in Belgium in 1988 and 1989. He formed John Jasperse Company in 1990.

Jasperse's work is often spoken of in oppositional pairs: violent and tender, awkward and precise, classical and vulgar. The most central counterpoint, however, occurs in the interplay between his tightly conceived structures and his elusive movement style. Jasperse often arrives at material by working out specific movement problems together with his dancers. Because of this interactive choreographic process, his dancers become intimately engaged in a deeply physical way: sharing each other's weight, supporting, carrying, pushing, and displacing one another in sequences of action and reaction. Jasperse challenges himself to confront his own discomforts, which means his work generates a certain amount of discomfort in the audience as well. In a rhythmic little dance of breasts and cocks, he and his dancers are utterly exposed. But his quiet, dry wit tempers our shock. Nothing in Jasperse's work is decorative. Sets are designed to be integral to the dance. Books are carried, stacked, tucked into armpits and mouths; ceilings descend and all but eliminate the dance space; rubber flooring rises and ebbs in oceanic waves. Some think of

Jasperse as cerebral, but the solutions to the puzzles he sets for himself are often wry and always theatrically apt.

Jasperse has had commissions from Baryshnikov's White Oak Dance Project, the Batsheva Dance Company in Tel Aviv, and the Lyon Opera Ballet. He has been granted fellowships from the John Simon Guggenheim Foundation, the National Endowment for the Arts, and the New York Foundation for the Arts. He has received the Choreography Prize of the Suzanne Dellal International Dance Competition in Tel Aviv, awards from the Künstlerhaus Mousonturm in Frankfurt, and three prizes at the Rencontres Internationales Chorégraphiques de Bagnolet.

* * *

John Jasperse in *Giant Empty* (photo Ross Taylor)

John Jasperse

When I was in high school in Rockville, Maryland, outside of Washington, D.C., I took an interest in combining singing and theater with my classical piano training and had the idea that musical theater would bring these interests together. But for that I needed dance. I mostly studied dance outside of school because the stigma of being a guy in the high school dance program was a bit much in the beginning. I decided to take dance composition and a Graham class. Clearly I had an odd idea about what was useful for musical theater.

I went to Sarah Lawrence College in the early eighties and studied the traditional modern dance techniques of Limón and Farber-style Cunningham. I also studied with Phyllis Lamhut, so I got a German influence as well. One summer during college I produced my own dance concert with a colleague at the Dance Place in D.C. Then in my junior year, when I was living in France, I saw the work of Trisha Brown and was blown away. Her use of the group and her complex manipulations of structure and space had a kind of purity. I knew then that I wanted to be a choreographer. I thought, "This is it! This is what I want to do."

When I came back to the States I was obsessed with getting into Trisha's company. Cunningham technique had always been a struggle for me but her movement vocabulary felt like it corresponded to what I thought my body could do well. I never got into her company, which probably in the end was a good thing for me because as a result I used the context of making my own work to try to figure out the ideas that interested me. After two or three years of making work that was basically Trisha rip-off, I had to address the questions: Who am I? and How can I integrate all of the ideas I've been playing with into something that has more to do with me?

I saw in Trisha's work an exploration of a certain softness and a symbiosis between people slipping against one another, grounded in forms that would magically fit together. That was so different from who I was, living in New York City, running around completely stressed out and anxious. I needed to find a way to integrate those aspects of myself that seemed perhaps negative, to find a place for them in the work so that I could figure them out. I also had to explore my own movement range. As a tall, thin man, I had experienced other people's expectations of what someone with this body would do. But early on in New York I worked a lot with Jennifer Monson, who encouraged shattering those expectations. She encouraged people who were seen as delicate to be completely bold and reckless. That gave me a new place to work from.

Then I got a job with Ann Teresa de Keersmaeker's company, Rosas, and went back and forth to Belgium for about two years, doing a project of hers and having a reencounter with Europe after five years away. I connected to a late-eighties European dance theater and the Belgian scene. Here in the States everything was about form, whereas there everything was about emotion. But soon thereafter there emerged a younger generation in Europe that was making a nondance antitheatrical kind of work that was a critical response to the European dance theater. I started to feel a kind of connection to all three: American postmodernism, European dance theater, and this reaction to European dance theater. I'm a bastard hybrid in terms of the schools of thought that have shaped my work.

I don't usually go into the studio alone and make dance phrases and then teach them. I make the material mostly when the dancers are there. Often material is created from some preconceived structure that guides the physical choices. We have a phrase from *Waving to you from here* from 1997 that we called "hypertwist" that's all about trying to do the most extreme reversing spirals that we can manage, one following the other. That material was created in one of the typical ways I make choreography, working in painstaking micro-increments, in this case trying out different radical twists. It is a process that is both physical and analytical, so I'm simultaneously doing and watching myself.

At other times making phrases is more intuitive, where I feel like trying a certain movement and I trust the feeling without knowing why. Later I might decide, no, that was just some weird desire of the moment; I needed to try out that movement but it doesn't need to be in the piece. But often I find that a coherence emerges that is not guided solely by intellect, and I am increasingly interested in this.

That said, I recognize in myself a proclivity to dance a certain way. People have called my movement awkward, functional, meticulously designed, loose yet precise—so it's not just one thing. I've understood a certain kind of physical language, which in turn has had a huge effect on my process. Recently when we were starting to make material, I stopped and thought, "Yeah, I recognize that as a nice, complicated, John Jasperse thing." I've been trying lately to figure out ways of subverting that identifiable style, trying to make choices in which my movement predispositions get removed from the picture. But in order to suspend my usual choices, I often have to bring in a really complicated game structure, some kind of puzzle that I'm trying to solve. Otherwise, the first thing that occurs to me if I give myself free rein is, perfectly naturally, what I already know. To get around that I might say to the dancers that everyone has to choose some portion of the next move and then—within a certain set of guidelines—we have to figure out a way that all of those choices can happen at the same time. Of course sometimes it's impossible. So then there's a compromise: How are we going to try and get as close to that combination as possible while yielding something that I would never have chosen to do? We try working with what we've each come up with and see where it evolves. We might see that it doesn't work at all. Or we might like some little sequence, for whatever reason, something interesting that has emerged from hazard, and we might pursue that. Since it exists as an object, I can choose it and say, "Okay, I want to put that object in," knowing that it's rubbing against my own aesthetic proclivities—and liking that.

Improvising with my dancers has often been physiologically based. For example, we've played with the idea of ball-and-socket joints. Your abdomen or some other part of your body that can create a concave surface can be like a socket for the ball of somebody else's body. We were constantly reforming the articulations between one body and another. Some of the problems would have to do with contrary impulses, like you try and do this while you also make a decision about what you want the other person to do. But they come in with their own idea about what they're trying to get you to do, and then it's about resolving these issues. But still I feel it's more physiological. It's not psychological or metaphysical.

Up to *Giant Empty*, which we premiered in Frankfurt in 2001 and then did at the Brooklyn Academy of Music, I had been working with the same three dancers and myself pretty much for six years. We had become a very tight-knit, intimate, but also slightly dysfunctional family. We did a lot of improvisation—but always with the onus of moving toward set choreography. The improvisation would be going fine, but once we began to set the choreography, subtle battles among us would ensue. Supposedly we had all experienced some moment together in the genesis of the material. But then everybody would sort out everybody else's memory of what that material was. Understandably, the dancers wanted to comprehend the material in relation to fixed points. But since the material was just starting to come into existence, I sometimes wondered how any of us could have a sense yet of what it was. It was difficult to figure out how to create a space where the theme was free to change and evolve, without feeling like we had to hold on to what it was.

When we were making all this dance material for *Giant Empty*, a conflict started emerging. Miguel Gutierrez, who was working with me at the time, was questioning me: "What are we doing with all of this dance material? I thought that you wanted to investigate fragile intuitive states and now we're making all these steps. What does that have to do with anything?" He had a point. I suppose that traditionally choreography has been very much about placing form on a higher plane and then everything else moving down from that. In making *Giant Empty*, I was interested in being less taken by what I could do with form and more taken by what I could do with the performative state of the dancers and the evolution of that state.

While I was thinking about this performative issue, I also was lined up to go to Japan to teach. I had never studied Butoh. I figured, "Why not apply for an Artists Exploration Fund and try to study with the Butoh master Kazuo Ohno? "Let's face it, he's in his nineties and he's not going to be around for very much longer." I was told, "You're not going to be able to study with Kazuo Ohno. You can study with his son Yoshito, but Kazuo doesn't go to the studio." His health was unstable. One month he'd be in the hospital and they'd think, "This is it, it's the end," and the next month he'd come out and go to the studio and do a performance.

So I went to Japan and, as it turns out, Kazuo was in relatively good health. Yoshito taught and Kazuo attended class. From what I've heard, Kazuo never taught in the way we know it. He'd speak about art and life and then everyone would improvise together. I also studied with Butoh artist Akira Kasai. I wasn't trying to do Butoh dance, but trying to understand a little bit about somebody else's tradition that was focused in another way. It seemed to me that in Butoh the performative aspect was really at the center. Even though it's from a perspective that's more metaphysical and unlike the way I might think about it, it was this performative aspect that drew me to it.

As it turned out, after *Giant Empty* Miguel Gutierrez and Parker Lutz decided to leave the company. That was a big shift. But it also meant I could examine how those relationships had functioned and say, "Okay, if I'm going to go forward and I'm going to construct something else, how can I be informed by what has happened?" Instead of just replicating the company with a carbon copy of more or less the same dancers, I had to let that go and ask, "Okay, what do I want to do now?"

I think it would have been a mistake to try and hold on to the old group. The group had its birth, its growth, its fleshy part, and its death. This change is just another part of life that has its own cycle. And that isn't necessarily bad; it's just the way it is. I've hired some new dancers. It'll be interesting to see what happens in initiating a relationship with people I don't know. There'll be lots to discover. In the commissions I've had over the past few years I've found a lot more richness in the process of working with other groups of dancers than I had originally imagined I would.

Meanwhile I'm doing a new duet with Juliette Mapp, called *just two dancers*. She and I know each other really well as people, as dancers, and as artists. Actually, I think you can get too comfortable. My rehearsal process with Juliette is just talk, talk, talk, talk, talk, talk, talk. She did an interview in *Time Out* where she said, "We always talked, but now we *really* talk!" I talk a lot with other people too; I talk in order to process ideas. For me the interesting thoughts come from discussion, not solely from inside of me. Since my gestural language and movement language tend to be limited by my own predisposition, I feel like my own little pea brain needs a lot of help. When the pea brain is enclosed inside of itself and the world gets shut out, certain underlying thoughts don't come up. Encounters with the world—people and objects—help bring them to consciousness. It's important to note that this discussion happens partly in words, but also profoundly in the physical exchange of dancing together.

just two dancers was never supposed to exist. We were supposed to do a repertory season this year at Dance Theater Workshop. But once two of my dancers decided to leave, I didn't want to backpedal and spend all that energy trying to teach the repertory to new people, especially since a lot of that rep, from a business perspective, felt like it didn't have that much of a sales life left to it. I would be doing it for one gig, which felt ridiculous. I knew we should do something else. It also seemed like we should take advantage of DTW as a performance venue that offers specific opportunities. We had done a certain kind of work for the "emblematic" opportunities that had come up, like Brooklyn Academy of Music and the commission for Lyon Opera Ballet, where I worked on a big scale. At BAM it is more difficult to go into the project feeling like, "I'm just going to do a crazy experiment! Maybe it's going to be a disaster." But it's important for me to realize that those big performances are not any more important than anything else. DTW is an opportunity to be a little more risky. That's what the DTW environment is supposed to be about.

I think part of the problem is that, in the decimation of the dance economy, venues like The Kitchen, DTW, Danspace, and P.S. 122 have turned into something other than they were originally intended to be. So now everyone wants to do the big, right thing there, too. I'd like to think I'm part of a movement interested in ripping down the idea of there being anything like the big, right thing. At least I need to take the opportunities that I feel are less high pressure where I can explore whatever I want to. And that ranges from doing somebody's benefit in a loft with an audience of twenty people, to small improvisational performances, to DTW with an audience of hundreds, to a large venue like the Brooklyn Academy of Music and, to the degree possible, to try and not differentiate between those contexts, between the "important" and the "unimportant." To realize that the weird performance with twenty people in somebody's living room may aesthetically have more importance in the development of my work than the show at BAM, in some perverse way, because it allows the opportunity for something new to happen. And unless there's that freedom to be disastrous and completely uninteresting I feel that there's also not as much ability to change and evolve and develop. And that's key.

Now that I seem to be moving into more prominence I think a lot about how to keep that sense of experimentation alive. In part it has to do with the structure of the organization that I build or choose to work in, which informs the identity of the work I make. Having a structure like a company should service the work, not the other way around. It's hard to figure out because, in the nature of things, you tend to move on in a pre-defined direction. If you're Merce Cunningham, you don't do little weird performances for twenty people who come over to a friend's loft.

To some degree *just two dancers* isn't quite as crazy as I originally imagined it. But in some way I feel like there was a willingness to take a strong risk at least on the format of the performance. I didn't know if it was going to work, but at some point I said, "This is what we're doing and there's no turning back." To me it's always in those harebrained ideas or the more extreme ideas that I start to see the real connections because they're floating much more on the surface. Okay, here's this extreme choice that we've made and that creates all of these different problems that are in your face right away. So how are we going to solve those problems?

One extreme choice for this piece is that we don't really dance on the stage. Part of that decision was due to my response to the architecture of the new theater. It was amazing that DTW got all this money together in a climate where it's so difficult to get any money and was able to do major reconstruction. But I was confused by some of their choices about the physical architecture of the theater. They have a poured concrete seating unit with theater seats that are bolted into the poured concrete. I felt shocked when I found that out and I thought what a huge assumption they're making about what people are doing now, which I don't even feel is correct, and about what people are going to do for the next twenty-five, thirty, or forty years. Here's this space that's supposed to be for the future and I'm not even convinced that it's addressing the present. How much more static a reification of these thoughts could we have than to pour concrete?

It seemed like a huge symbol to me and I felt like I needed to respond to it. I didn't want people to walk in and, without thinking, sit down in their seats and just accept the reification of these assumptions. I felt like I needed to point to this and say, "Something really weird is happening here." And not only at DTW because, as it turned out, the entire world seems to be revolving around certain assumptions about what truth is and what we should do in the world and how we should treat people. I wondered, "Are we really paying attention?" I felt that there was a parallel between how the architecture was proposing certain kinds of ideas and how the media and the world and the powers that be were proposing certain kinds of ideas. That said, I then made a decision: The audience is facing front but we're going to dance behind them!

So that was a huge problem. A lot of thought went into trying to figure out how to get people to see the dance. Then the whole question arose whether this piece is really about them seeing it. Or is it about them knowing that there are things happening that they can't see? So broader issues came up because of a harebrained idea that flew in the face of everything that seemed to be correct.

Every audience member of *just two dancers* has an individual mirror. They get to create their own composition of what we're doing and each see something different. By giving everyone a device that can define their field of vision, I'm basically disempowering myself in making the choreography. I don't control it in the way that I can in a proscenium space where everybody is looking forward and the architecture is framing what they see. The setup with the mirrors blew all of that out of the water from the beginning. We're pointing people to ask themselves questions about how they're looking and how they understand what they see because of how they are looking. It's a critique about prepackaged information that is given to us to explain an event.

Most of my choreography can be seen as a projection of my mind onto the object of the work. At least for this moment, in this piece, I'm making a shift. *just two dancers* is about form, but it's also about the dissolution of form. In making this piece, we're trying out some new processes in the hope of exploring ideas without needing to know so quickly what they are. To give an example, we've used different scores including "dance for yourself," "dance for somebody else's vision," and "dance for the mirror." We're differentiating between these states and I'm trying to reexamine what that might yield. We're also working with internal motivations. We have a score that involves our imagining certain physical materials and then imagining that we're drawing on our body with those materials. They can change from a feather, to a lit blowtorch, to honey, to any material that elicits some kind of physiological response to that imagined material. Of course, nobody is going to see that that's what we're doing. That's not important to me. But the process leads to a dynamic form because the form is really about our response.

Juliette and I started by improvising and as that process progressed it didn't seem clear why we should set the movement. So now, instead of clamping down on an idea, we just let it run around the studio wildly and try and observe it as it's happening in us. At the end of the day we can leave the studio and not have any notion what we're going to do with it. Our improvising together in the new piece is really about the transmission of information to each other. If we knew what the other was doing, we would no longer be trying to figure it out, so we had to leave it open. Showing the process of discovery, the questioning, and the attempt to understand is more interesting to me at the current moment than showing a static object that we want the audience to see and understand.

That's been a progression in my work from pieces like *Waving to you from here* in 1997, where I wanted people to understand something specific and I wanted the meaning to be legible. Then afterwards I realized, "Hmm, there's something about dance that is inherently ambiguous. There's a plurality of meanings." The fact that there isn't a Cartesian fixed meaning is actually a power rather than a problem. One of the powers of dance has to do with the way in which individual spectators bring themselves to that collection of ambiguities and try to make sense out of this thing that is not easily legible. By trying to force dance into a form that is comprehensible in one fixed manner, a lot of rich stuff gets squeezed out of the picture.

Already with my dance *Madison as I imagine it* in 1999, I started to incorporate that ambiguity more purposefully into the work and not to have my voice as choreographer so prominently telling the audience what to think. I wanted to have meaning that was more porous and left more space for the viewers individually to construct their own meaning from what I'm giving them. I feel like the duet *just two dancers* is a further extension of what I did in *Madison* and in *Giant Empty*. It's an invitation for the audience to be active participants. They actually have to make physical choices—and not just intellectual ones—about what they will see.

My work with scenic designers hasn't always been smooth sailing, but perhaps that has led to interesting products. For *Giant Empty* I worked with scenic artist Matthias Bringmann. We started discussing the abstract concepts of the work before I'd even started rehearsing. I felt like there were some issues in my earlier piece *Fort Blossom* that that I wanted to continue to explore—ideas about creating borders and changing borders and how groups get formed and how they dissolve. Then Matthias came up with six or seven preliminary ideas that he sent me on a CD-ROM. I didn't like any of them. Matthias would bring in objects that would be conceptually related to my ideas, but I didn't know what to do with them. Why were they there? Were they just another manifestation of the concepts we had talked about? That became really puzzling and difficult for us to try and figure out. So we began a long process of trying to sort through all of that.

The use of the blocks in that piece was an evolution from junk that just happened to be around, not from an imposed idea. The company was in a studio away from New York where the only source of heat was a wood-burning stove, so there was a log pile right there. I was thinking maybe we could do something like balancing with the wood, connecting to an idea about fragility. So we brought the logs out into the studio and we tried all this stuff and we ended up doing seated movements balanced on these logs. I originally intended for them to be in the piece. But when we came back to New York there were no logs, so I thought maybe we should just get four-by-four lumber, which we did. Matthias cut them up and brought them to the studio and we continued working with them. And that's how they got included. The only reference to the balancing on the logs is the walking that Juliette does across the line of blocks at the opening of the show. But we chose that junk for a reason and I hope the original reasons that drew us to it continue to resonate.

With an outside designer I feel tension in the design process. It has made me feel more and more like I need to go back to designing my own shows. Making *Waving to you from here* in 1997, I was working in quite a large studio in Grenoble. One side of it had a low roof with a truss that went across and supported the low part. The bottom of the truss was at seven-and-a-half or eight feet. I was dancing and I turned around quickly and almost whacked my hand on this truss. That incident led me to come up with the idea of a collapsing ceiling that would descend. We could interact with it. But this notion began really just from chance—some set of circumstances that was not planned at all hit against the larger set of ideas that I had been thinking about.

Another example of serendipity occurred when I was in Dublin in fall 2002 making a commission for John Scott's Irish Modern Dance Theatre. We were making new material and were dealing with round objects. I felt like there needed to be something with angles. I looked around the room and saw chairs. Then those chairs became a central item. They were objects that were symbolic of rest, designed to conform to the body, to support it in an alert but rested position, and yet we used them in a way in which they were totally unfriendly to the body. The piece was called *Misfit*.

Because the expected symbiotic relationship never comes about, a tension results. But I never would just have had the idea of using chairs. They got used because there were three hundred chairs sitting over on the side of the studio. And that's been true pretty much throughout my process. I feel like the detritus of stuff around me, whether it be ideas or objects or something that rubs against what I'm thinking at the moment, suddenly makes a third object that's bigger than what my designer said and bigger than what I was thinking and leads us somewhere that neither of us could have gone alone. And that to me is successful collaboration.

I've made four pieces together with the composer James Lo. We had a great fusion going. When I started collaborating with James, I was working on a piece with a table, called *Furnished/Unfurnished*, which premiered in 1993. The table generated a lot of sound that I felt couldn't coexist very well with traditional music. I needed to have someone deal with these sounds. I was referred to James and he did a great job. He dealt with a lot of found sounds which, mostly after the fact, I realized were functioning in a really interesting way. They contextualized a lot of the visual input that would otherwise be abstract and gave it concrete associations—in much the same way that the props or certain aspects of the movement did. So they allowed us to exist in an abstract soup that now had real things floating in it. We could give the audience some life preservers to hold on to, which could make the experience of being inside the abstraction more comfortable and more comprehensible.

I would develop a lot of movement material and then James would come in and we'd start to figure out how we were going to address these events. And so the score was constructed as a function of the development of the dancing. In some cases, the choreography was almost finished before the score began to come in. With *Scrawl* in 1999, however, we had a very short time frame. We had to make a piece in seven weeks. He wouldn't have had enough time if he waited until I had done my part, so we had to work concurrently. By doing it this way, the music was not made to support the dance in the way that it had before. Rather than him responding to me, there was a sense of how the two would create a dynamic interplay; rather than the one accompanying the other, they coexisted in some kind of interrelationship where each was more independent.

I also made a piece with composer Han Rowe, who was working with manipulated acoustic instrumentation. From there I began collaborating more and more with people working in the electronic genre, so the sounds became much less concrete, much less referable.

Waving to You from Here by John Jasperse (photo Maria Anguera de Sojo)

Fort Blossom by John Jasperse (photo Maria Anguera de Sojo)

When I made a piece for Baryshnikov's White Oak Project, they had originally been talking about the possibility of having a string quartet available to perform. Zenna Parkins, a composer friend of mine who has also written for me, suggested a Ligeti string quartet, which I loved. But then I thought, "Oh, I can't make a dance to this. It's way too much a particular genre, 1960s modernist." It felt like the quartet should be performed by women in black jersey dresses, sawing away on the strings. I couldn't figure out how to reconcile a period that seemed so screaming mid-twentieth century with what I felt like I was doing. So instead I collaborated with Stephen Vitiello on the White Oak Project. But then I went back to the Ligeti and used it for my commission from American Dance Festival and for another piece as well. I'm also using some other pieces of Ligeti from the same period, roughly 1968, which are similar in genre. I had never before made anything to that kind of music.

I was really excited by the complexity of the music's compositional form and how it related to what I was doing in a more rhythmic way than I had been used to. The complexity of the rhythmic changes in that particular instance created a heightened, energetic environment in which the dance took place. Even though I feel like rhythm and phrasing have been central in my movement, we never choreographed with those being the first plane. The design aspect of the movement would generally take the more primary place, then phrasing would come after our understanding of what we were dealing with in terms of task, design, and visual form. Now with *just two dancers* we improvise a lot and we're not trying to set form in the same way, so there's the possibility of working with the rhythms in a more complicated manner.

When I'm beginning a new project, there's often a long time where I feel like a charlatan, like I'm just making up stuff to do, because I don't really understand what we're doing. As I've gotten older I've tried to trust that there is an intuitive intelligence that will emerge into something that's coherent. But I feel a lot of internal resistance, too: "Well, why do that? I mean, sure we could do that, but we could do that other thing, too. So why do anything?" That's a real battle for me.

But in the midst of it all there are moments when exchanges happen that are great, when you see something that you haven't ever seen, or when you're hit by the laughter or the craziness. I love that. And I find there are moments when I go into the studio when I've been in a bad mood and it turns out that I can transform that feeling and forget about the petty problems of my individual life and think about the dance I'm doing that, for some strange reason, I find magical. Making the material gets me curious or interested or it makes me laugh. Juliette and I will sometimes marvel, "Can you believe that this is what we do for a living?" We go into the room and we spend hours doing crazy, weird shit. That's great.

Somewhere toward the end of making a piece I'm usually convinced that this one is just going to suck. But it's too late to go back. There were a couple of weeks working on the new piece when I was wondering, "Have we really lost our minds? We're going to improvise for an hour; we're not going to dance on the stage; people can't even see the piece. Why would anyone be interested in this?" But I figured, "Okay, maybe it's going to be a disaster." With every dance I say the same thing: "This might be the one that just sucks." I suppose this tells you more about my personal psychology than about the work itself. I don't know why I haven't quite figured out that they all somehow pull through in the end.

I'm thinking a lot about the structure of the company, the structure in which I work, in relation to the development of my career. Where do I want the work to go and how can I keep it alive? All those questions about diffusion, dissemination, touring, company structure, commissions. Is it dance? Is it not dance? How do other elements enter into it? These seem to be the real questions right now. Yet I feel resistant to trying to set a model. Having lost two of my dancers, I have the opportunity to restructure. But the current context is such a problem. The funding picture is falling apart even worse than before. And it's difficult to attract an audience and maintain a connection to the larger culture, to society.

When I start to see: this is John Jasperse, or this is the John Jasperse Company, or this what I do, or this is what we do—then I'm feeling a voice in the back of my head saying that once you can identify any of that, it's time to stop doing it and to start trying to do something else. Otherwise we have the bundt-cake form and we just keep having to pour more batter into it, shove it into the oven, and pull out another cake. I've certainly seen examples of that kind of entropy. The only way you can try and combat that is by going back to the organizational structure itself. Once that structure is static, it's going to say, "This is what we're set up to do, so we can't do that other thing." That's the time to rip the organization apart and try and reform it. Or you have to try and create it in the first place in such a way that it's flexible enough to address those concerns. So, yes, the infrastructure and choreographic structure and form and aesthetic identity all are related one to another. I haven't fully figured that out and don't know that I ever will. Maybe it's impossible to figure out. By its nature something will always need to be chopped down and transformed. And ironically, one good thing about the instability of the current time is that change is my only option anyway.

New York City
May 18, 2003

Selected Bibliography

General and Background:

Banes, Sally. *Democracy's Body: Judson Dance Theater, 1962–1964.* Ann Arbor: UMI Research Press, 1983.

Banes, Sally. *Terpsichore in Sneakers: Post-Modern Dance.* Boston: Houghton Mifflin, 1980.

Banes, Sally. *Writing Dancing in the Age of Postmodernism.* Middletown, Conn.: Wesleyan University Press, 1994.

Bremser, Martha, ed. *Fifty Contemporary Choreographers.* London and New York: Routledge, 1999.

Dils, Ann, and Ann Cooper Albright. *A Dance History Reader: Moving History/Dancing Cultures.* Middletown, Conn.: Wesleyan University Press, 2001.

Foster, Susan Leigh. *Reading Dancing: Bodies and Subjects in Contemporary American Dance.* Berkeley: University of California Press, 1986.

Kreemer, Connie. *Further Steps: Fifteen Choreographers on Modern Dance.* New York: Harper & Row, 1987.

Ramsay, Margaret Hupp. *The Grand Union (1970–1976): An Improvisational Performance Group.* New York: Peter Lang, 1991.

Roseman, Janet Lynn. *Dance Masters: Interviews with Legends of Dance.* New York: Routledge, 2001.

Vergne, Phillippe, Siri Engberg, and Kellie Jones, curators. *Art Performs Life: Merce Cunningham, Meredith Monk, Bill T. Jones.* Minneapolis: Walker Art Center, 1998.

Individual Choreographers:

Trisha Brown:

Brown, Trisha. "Three Pieces." *The Drama Review* (March 1975): 26–31.

Goldberg, Marianne. Interview with Trisha Brown. "Trisha Brown: All of the Person's Arriving." *The Drama Review* (spring 1986): 149–70.

Howell, John, ed. "Trisha Brown: An Informal Performance." *Breakthroughs: Avant-Garde Artists in Europe and America 1950–1990.* New York: Rizzoli, 1991: 246–251.

Livet, Anne, ed. "Trisha Brown." *Contemporary Dance.* New York: Abbeville Press, 1978: 42–55.

Perron, Wendy. "Trisha Brown on Tour." *Dancing Times* (May 1996): 749–751.

Teicher, Hendel, ed. *Trisha Brown: Dance and Art in Dialogue, 1961–2001.* Boston: MIT Press, 2002.

Ann Carlson:

Hamlin, Jesse. " History Comes to Life." *The San Francisco Chronicle*, July 7, 2002, final edition: 39.
Lempert-Greaux, Ellen, and Amy L. Singerland. "Living Sculpture." *Lighting Dimensions* (September 2000): 32–38, 40.
O'Keefe, Maura. Jacob's Pillow: "Pillow Notes," July 9–12, 1998.
Perron, Wendy. "A Performance Piece Runs through It." *The New York Times*, August 10, 2003, late edition: 26.
Reardon, Christopher. "Laughter on the Hill." *The Village Voice*, July 14, 1998: 160.
Temin, Christine. "Going for a Spin." *The Boston Globe*, May 11, 2003, third edition: N1.
Weinstein, Tresca. "Pose Garden: Ann Carlson's *Night Light* Brings the Past to Life at Jacob's Pillow." *The Times Union* (Albany, N.Y.), July 26, 2001: 16.

Lucinda Childs:

Chin, Daryl. "Talking with Lucinda Childs." *Dance Scope* (winter-spring 1979): 70–81.
Fanger, Iris. "Lucinda Childs and *Parcours*." *Dance Magazine* (October 2000): 67–69.
Fanger, Iris. "The New Lucinda Childs." *Dance Magazine* (October 1989): 48–53.
Livet, Anne, ed. "Lucinda Childs." *Contemporary Dance*. New York: Abbeville Press, 1978: 58–81.
Sontag, Susan. "A Lexicon for *Available Light*." *Where the Stress Falls: Essays*. New York: Farrar, Straus, and Giroux, 2001: 161–177.

Merce Cunningham:

Copeland, Roger in *Merce Cunningham: The Modernizing of Modern Dance*. London and New York: Routledge, 2003.
Cunningham, Merce in conversation with Jacqueline Lesschaeve. *The Dancer and the Dance*. New York and London: Marion Boyars, 1985.
Klosty, James. *Merce Cunningham*. New York: Saturday Review Press, 1975.
Kostelanetz, Richard, ed. *Merce Cunningham: Dancing in Space and Time*. Pennington, N.J.: A Cappella Press, 1992.
Vaughan, David. *Merce Cunningham: Fifty Years*. New York: Aperture, 1999.
Vergne, Phillippe, Siri Engberg, and Kellie Jones, curators. *Art Performs Life*. Minneapolis: Walker Art Center, 1998: 16–65.

Eiko and Koma:

Carbonneau, Suzanne. "The Weight of History, the Lightness of the Universe." 2002 Bates Dance Festival. http://www.eikoandkoma.org/ekcarbonneau.html.
Dufton, Merry. "Eiko and Koma Interview." *New Dance* (January 1988): 15–17.
Josa-Jones, Paula. "Delicious Moving." *Contact Quarterly* (winter 1986): 11–15.
Mihopoulos, Effie. Interview with Eiko and Koma. *Salome*. 32–33 (1983): 91–105.
Windham, Leslie. "A Conversation with Eiko & Koma." *Ballet Review* (summer 1988): 47–59.

David Gordon:

Anderson, Jack. "Dancers Talk, but Can You Believe Them?" *The New York Times*, February 20, 2003, late edition: 5.
Croce, Arlene. "Making Work." *The New Yorker*, November, 29, 1982: 51–107.
Gordon, David. "It's About Time." *The Drama Review* (March 1975): 43–52.
Meisner, Nadine. "Reviews: Dance—David Gordon/Pick up Performance Company, the Place London." *The Independent* (London), November 8, 2001: 12.

Smith, Karen. "David Gordon's *The Matter.*" *The Drama Review* (September 1972): 117–127.
Weinstein, Tresca. "Dance Is His Life: David Gordon's *Private Lives* Incorporates the Quotidian." *The Times Union* (Albany, N.Y.), August 22, 2002: 40.

Anna Halprin:

Halprin, Anna. *Dance as a Healing Art: Returning to Health through Movement & Imagery.* Mendocino, Calif.: LifeRhythm, 2002.
Halprin, Anna. *Moving toward Life: Five Decades of Transformational Dance.* Edited by Rachel Kaplan. Hanover and London: Wesleyan University Press, 1995.
Ross, Janice. *Anna Halprin: Revolution for the Art of It.* Berkeley: University of California Press, forthcoming.

John Jasperse:

Harris, William. "Obsessed with a Vision of Existential Despair." *The New York Times,* May 2, 1999, late edition, section 2: 12.
Kern, Lauren. "Midwestern Dialect: With *Madison,* John Jasperse Images a Place where People Move in Mysterious Ways." *Houston Press* (Texas), April 13, 2000. http://www.houston-press.com/issues/2000-04-13/dance.html
Kisselgoff, Anna. "Next Wave Festival Review; Exposed to the Elements in an Existential No Man's Land." New York Times, November 16, 2001, late edition: section E: 8.
Kourlas, Gia. "Where Dance Is Moving: Off the Stage." *The New York Times,* July 27, 2003, late edition, section 2: 18.

Bill T. Jones:

Dixon Gottschild, Brenda. *The Black Dancing Body: A Geography from Coon to Cool.* New York: Palgrave-Macmillan, 2003.
Jones, Bill T., with Peggy Gillespie. *Last Night on Earth.* New York: Pantheon Books, 1995.
Jones, Bill T., and Arnie Zane. *Body against Body: The Dance and Other Collaborations.* Barrytown, N.Y.: Station Hill Press, 1989.
Lee, Albert. "Generations Find Place at Jones' Table." *Dance Magazine* (August 2001): 76–77.
Vergne, Phillippe, Siri Engberg, and Kellie Jones, curators. *Art Performs Life.* Minneapolis: Walker Art Center, 1998: 116–157.

Meredith Monk:

Baker, Rob. "New Worlds for Old: The Visionary Art of Meredith Monk." *American Theatre Magazine* (October 1984).
Jowitt, Deborah, ed. *Meredith Monk.* Baltimore: Johns Hopkins University Press, 1997.
Marranca, Bonnie. "Meredith Monk's Atlas of Sound: New Opera and the American Performance Tradition." *Ecologies of Theater: Essays at the Century Turning.* Baltimore: Johns Hopkins University Press, 1996: 224–232.
Satin, Leslie. "Being Danced Again: Meredith Monk, Reclaiming the Girlchild." In *Moving Words: Re-Writing Dance,* edited by Gay Morris. London and New York: Routledge, 1996: 121–140.
Siegel, Marcia B. "Evolutionary Dreams." *Dance Theatre Journal* (London) (October 1986): 2–5.
Vergne, Phillippe, Siri Engberg, and Kellie Jones, curators. *Art Performs Life.* Minneapolis: Walker Art Center, 1998: 66–115.

Mark Morris:

Acocella, Joan. *Mark Morris*. New York: Farrar, Straus, and Giroux, 1993.

Craine, Debra. "The Ruling Class: Twenty Years of Mark Morris." *Dance Now* (winter 2001): 67–73.

Morris, Gay. "Styles of the Flesh: Gender in the Dances of Mark Morris." In *Moving Words: Re-Writing Dance*, edited by Gay Morris. London and New York: Routledge, 1996: 141–158.

Ulrich, Allan. "Reviews: National: Morris's Musical *V* Inspires Pride." *Dance Magazine* (January 2002): 98.

Elizabeth Streb:

Anderson, Jack. "Choreography All Ready for the Scrimmage Line." *The New York Times*, June 4, 2002, late edition: E5.

Burns, Judy. "Wild Bodies/Wilder Minds: Streb/Ringside and Spectacle." *Women and Performance: A Journal of Feminist Theory* 7, no. 1 (1994): 97–121.

Dalva, Nancy. "Wham Bam Streb." *Dance Magazine* (June 2003): 21–23, 68.

Jowitt, Deborah. "Redefining Innovation." *The Village Voice*, September 6–12, 2000: 71.

Reigenborn, Garry D. "Elizabeth Streb: Movement in Time and Space." New York Academy of Sciences. http://www.nyas1.inetu.net/about/newsDetails.asp?news ID=37&year=2003.

Siegel, Marcia B. "Whammers: Streb Takes No Prisoners." *The Boston Phoenix*, January 8–15, 1998: 13.

Index